Cooking Italian

MAIN DISHES

THUNDER BAY
P·R·E·S·S

Editorial Director: Cristina Cappa Legora
Editorial Coordinator: Valeria Camaschella
Translation: Studio Traduzioni Vecchia, Milan
North American Edition
Managing Editor: JoAnn Padgett
Associate Editor: Elizabeth McNulty

Table of Contents

First published in the United States by

Thunder Bay Press
5880 Oberlin Drive, Suite 400
San Diego, CA 92121-4794
1-800-284-3580
http://www.advmkt.com

ISBN 1-57145-197-8

Library of Congress Cataloging-in-Publication Data available upon request

Printed in Singapore

1 2 3 4 5 99 00 01 02 03

Introduction

Cooking is a necessity and a pleasure. Or rather, necessity is transformed into pleasure. Today, we like to try out new ingredients whenever we can, inventing variations on traditional dishes, and experimenting with unusual types of cooking procedures.

This new series of books was designed to make cooking a pleasant pastime, with recipes based on our tradition that nevertheless often contain a little something extra, a flash of imagination, an exotic variation that makes the dish more appetizing and impressive.

The books you'll peruse will include a number of tools to help you achieve the best possible results without making mistakes or wasting time. First of all, look at the summary in each section, which will give you an immediate overview of the dishes included. The color illustrations will help you quickly choose the recipe you like best.

The recipes themselves are designed to be as practical as possible. The ingredients are clearly listed to the side, followed by the equipment necessary and a practical chart that summarizes everything you need to know right away, before you begin cooking: the degree of difficulty, preparation and cooking time, cooking method, how long the dish will keep, and so on. The description of the recipes is also extremely clear and detailed, and is divided into sections that cover each separate stage of the recipe.

Another important feature is the suggestion of an appropriate wine to be served with the dish. (These are just suggestions because we all know that wines are a matter of personal taste.) To make it easier for you, we have always selected wines with appellation contrôlée, with the official caption. Of course, we also provide the best temperature for serving each individual wine.

In addition, there are always practical, useful suggestions on the recipe itself (for example, whether you can change any ingredients, how to multiply a given dish), or related to preparation (for example, how to prevent ravioli from breaking as they cook).

Finally, we include a "special note" for each preparation—some extra information on an ingredient in the recipe that may be historical, scientific, dietetic and so forth—that further enriches the descriptions.

This book is devoted to MAIN DISHES and is full of tasty recipes, broken down according to their main ingredients: Pasta and Rice, Meat and Fish, and Vegetables. These are recipes that can serve as both a first and second course, something that's increasingly important today, when there is less time to cook.

Recipe Index

Rice with Croquettes p32

Rice with Eggs p33

Rice and Zucchini Mold p34

Sicilian Risotto p36

Rice with Onions p38

Exotic Paella p40

Risotto with Tench p42

Rice Pilaf with Curry p44

Risotto alla Pavese p45

Pasta and Rice

Macaroni dei Borboni

INGREDIENTS
serves 4–6

3/4 lb. – 300 g FRESH EGG PASTA DOUGH,
already prepared
SALT and PEPPER to taste
1 1/2 lb. – 600 g TOMATOES
4 tablespoons EXTRA VIRGIN OLIVE OIL
1 ONION
2 oz. – 1 bunch CALAMINT (basil thyme)
or basil
1 BAY leaf
1 SAGE leaf
1 sprig MARJORAM
1 pinch SUGAR
3/4 lb. – 300 g MOZZARELLA
4 tablespoons GRATED PARMESAN

EQUIPMENT
a pot
a saucepan
a baking dish

Difficulty	AVERAGE
Preparation Time	30 MIN.
Cooking Time	40 MIN.
Method of cooking	STOVETOP AND OVEN
Microwave	YES
Freezing	YES
Keeping Time	3 DAYS

SPECIAL NOTE
Marjoram is not only used for cooking, but can also be used to flavor lemon juice — just add two leaves of fresh marjoram.

RECOMMENDED WINES
Capri bianco (Campania): dry white wine served at 50°F / 10°C
Sicilian Sambuca Chardonnay (Sicily):
mellow, aromatic white wine served at 50°F / 10°C

1 Roll the dough out in thin layers, cut into strips 1.5 inches – 4 cm wide and 4.5 inches – 12 cm long. Cook a few at a time in a pot with a generous amount of salted boiling water. Drain as soon as they rise to the surface and place on a damp towel.

2 In the meantime, prepare the sauce. Scald the tomatoes in boiling water for a minute, remove the skin and seeds, and mince the pulp coarsely. Place 2 tablespoons oil in a saucepan and add the finely minced onion, half the calamint, the bay leaf, the sage and the marjoram. Heat over low heat to wilt the onion without browning it. Add the tomatoes, a pinch of salt and pepper and the sugar. Cook over moderate heat and reduce the sauce. Finally, add the rest of the calamint and remaining oil, mix and remove immediately from the heat. Cut the mozzarella into strips.

3 Spread a tablespoon sauce in the baking dish, place a layer of pasta on top, and on this spread 2 tablespoons sauce. Arrange a few strips of mozzarella and sprinkle with a bit of grated parmesan. Continue the same procedure until the ingredients are finished, ending with a layer of sauce and mozzarella, and sprinkling with grated parmesan. Place the dish in a preheated 375° oven and cook the "macaroni" for 20 minutes. Serve hot.

PRACTICAL SUGGESTIONS
To speed up preparation time, we have suggested already prepared pasta dough. If you prefer, you can make it yourself, using 1/2 lb. – 200 g flour, 2 eggs, a tablespoon extra virgin olive oil and a pinch of salt.

8

Spaghetti alla Bizzarra

1 Clean the eggplants, wash them, dry them, chop and place them in a colander. Sprinkle with a pinch of salt and let them sit for 30 minutes to lose some of their vegetable liquid.

2 Scald the plum tomatoes for a few moments in a pot of boiling water, drain, remove the skin and seeds and slice. Finely mince the onion with the clove of garlic, place the mixture in a skillet, add the oil and let it brown gently.

3 Add the cubed eggplant (which you have previously rinsed and dried), mix again and fry for 10 minutes. Add the sliced tomatoes, season with a pinch of salt, a bit of freshly ground pepper, and finish cooking the sauce over moderate heat for another 20 minutes.

4 Five minutes before removing from the heat, add the crumbled, drained tuna and the minced basil leaves. Cook the pasta in a pot with a generous amount of salted boiling water, drain when al dente, transfer the spaghetti to a heated serving dish, season it with the prepared sauce and add the cubed fontina. Stir again and serve immediately.

PRACTICAL SUGGESTIONS
To give this dish a touch of extra color, add a half a packet of saffron to the pasta cooking water and garnish the serving dish with several slices of fresh tomato.

INGREDIENTS

serves 4

2 EGGPLANTS
SALT and PEPPER to taste
1 lb. – 400 g PLUM TOMATOES
1 ONION
1 clove GARLIC
4 tablespoons EXTRA VIRGIN OLIVE OIL
1/4 lb. – 110 g TUNA PACKED IN OIL
2 oz. – 1 bunch BASIL
1 lb. – 400 g SPAGHETTI
1/4 lb. FONTINA CHEESE, cubed

EQUIPMENT

2 pots
a skillet
a serving dish

Difficulty	**AVERAGE**
Preparation Time	**15 MIN. + 30 MIN.**
Cooking Time	**45 MIN.**
Method of cooking	**STOVETOP**
Microwave	**NO**
Freezing	**NO**
Keeping Time	**2 DAYS**

SPECIAL NOTE

Several similar species are sold under the generic name of tuna, including long–fin tuna, whose flesh is highly prized, and false albacore, which is not as high quality.

Baked Pennette with Mozzarella

INGREDIENTS

serves 4

1 lb. – 400 g firm, ripe TOMATOES
1 ONION
4 tablespoons EXTRA VIRGIN OLIVE OIL
3/4 lb. – 300 g SHELLED PEAS
SALT and PEPPER to taste
2 oz. – 1 bunch BASIL
1 lb. – 400 g PENNETTE
(a short, tubular pasta)
1 FRESH MOZZARELLA weighing about
1/2 lb. – 200 g
4 tablespoons GRATED PARMESAN

For the baking dish
1 tablespoon EXTRA VIRGIN OLIVE OIL

EQUIPMENT

a saucepan
a pot
a baking dish

Difficulty	**AVERAGE**
Preparation Time	**20 MIN.**
Cooking Time	**40 MIN.**
Method of cooking	**STOVETOP AND OVEN**
Microwave	**YES**
Freezing	**YES**
Keeping Time	**2 DAYS**

SPECIAL NOTE

The origin of pasta is very uncertain. Some archaeologists believe they have found traces of equipment and paintings regarding pasta, but more concrete evidence comes from China.

RECOMMENDED WINES
Friuli Grave rosato (Friuli Venezia Giulia): rosé served at 50°F / 10°C
Parrina rosato (Tuscany): rosé served at 50°F / 10°C

1 Scald the tomatoes in boiling water, remove the skin and seeds and coarsely chop the pulp. Finely mince the onion and wilt it in a saucepan with the oil. Add the minced tomato pulp, the peas, a pinch of salt and pepper and cook for 15–20 minutes. Before removing from the heat, add the basil leaves, cut into strips.

2 Boil a generous amount of salted water in a pot, cook the pennette and drain when very al dente. Season with a third of the tomato sauce and peas, half the mozzarella chopped into pieces and a bit of grated parmesan.

3 In an oiled baking dish, spread half the pennette in a single layer. Drizzle with a bit of tomato sauce, add·part of the mozzarella and sprinkle with grated parmesan.

4 Cover with the rest of the pennette and repeat the above–described operation. Place the baking dish in an oven pre–heated to 400°F and bake the pennette about 10–12 minutes, until the surface is browned, then serve piping hot.

PRACTICAL SUGGESTIONS
When you add pasta to water, the water temperature lowers. Turn up the heat immediately to start it boiling again, then lower it so the water stays at a constant simmer. Pasta should cook uncovered.

Macaroni alla Chitarra with Sauce

INGREDIENTS

serves 4–6

1 lb. – 400 g DURUM WHEAT FLOUR
2 EGG WHITES
SALT to taste

For the sauce

1/4 lb. – 100 g BONELESS PORK
1/4 lb. – 100 g BONELESS VEAL
2 oz. – 50 g LEAN BACON, in one piece
half an ONION, 1 CARROT
1 stalk CELERY
3 tablespoons EXTRA VIRGIN OLIVE OIL
SALT and PEPPER to taste
1/2 cup DRY WHITE WINE
1 HOT PEPPER
2 tablespoons GRATED PECORINO

EQUIPMENT

a rolling pin, a *chitarra* (pasta frame)
a skillet, a pot, a serving dish

Difficulty	AVERAGE
Preparation Time	40 MIN. + 30 MIN.
Cooking Time	1 HOUR 20 MIN.
Method of cooking	STOVETOP
Microwave	NO
Freezing	YES
Keeping Time	2 DAYS

SPECIAL NOTE

The *chitarra* is a traditional tool from Abruzzo that is used to prepare tagliatelle known as macaroni. It is made of a wooden frame strung with steel wires nailed across it.

RECOMMENDED WINES
Montepulciano d'Abruzzo (Abruzzi): light red wine served at 64°F / 18°C
Valpolicella (Veneto): light red wine served at 61°F / 16°C

1 Sift the flour onto a flat surface and mound. Place the egg whites in the center, along with a bit of salt and enough water to make a smooth, uniform dough. Wrap it in plastic wrap and let it rest for 30 minutes. Then roll it out into a sheet about 1/8 inch – 3 mm thick, cut into strips the size of the *chitarra*, flour them, place them on the *chitarra* one at a time and roll the rolling pin over them. Press firmly so the macaroni will fall onto the cutting board.

2 Prepare the sauce. Finely mince the pork and veal, and mince the bacon as well. Peel the onion, trim, the carrot and peel it, and remove the threads from the celery. Heat the oil in a skillet, add the bacon, and sauté. Add the onion, the celery and the carrot and wilt them, stirring occasionally with a wooden spoon. Add the minced meats and sauté over high heat until they are browned on all sides. Add salt and pepper, pour in the wine and allow it to evaporate. Finally, add the hot pepper and cook the sauce over moderate heat for an hour, covered.

3 In the meantime, cook the macaroni *alla chitarra* in a pot with a generous amount of salted boiling water, drain al dente and season with the prepared sauce. Place it in a serving dish and serve hot immediately.

PRACTICAL SUGGESTIONS
If you don't have a chitarra, you can prepare these macaroni by rolling the pasta and cutting it into strips 1/8 inch wide, which you should spread on a dry dishtowel and allow to dry.

Taglierini Soup with Vegetables

INGREDIENTS
serves 4

1 TURNIP
SALT to taste
3/4 lb. – 300 g SAVOY CABBAGE
2 CARROTS
2 ZUCCHINI
2 stalks CELERY
1 LEEK
1/3 lb. – 150 g SHELLED PEAS
1 clove GARLIC
1.5 oz. – 30 g DRY MUSHROOMS,
already softened
1 firm, ripe TOMATO
1 SALTED ANCHOVY
2 tablespoons EXTRA VIRGIN OLIVE OIL
1/2 lb. – 200 g TAGLIERINI

EQUIPMENT
2 pots, a bowl
a small saucepan, a saucepan

Difficulty	**AVERAGE**
Preparation Time	**35 MIN. + 20 MIN.**
Cooking Time	**1 HOUR 10 MIN.**
Method of cooking	**STOVETOP**
Microwave	**NO**
Freezing	**NO**
Keeping Time	**1 DAY**

SPECIAL NOTE
Turnips were very important in the diet of central and northern Europe, at least until potatoes and maize were imported.

RECOMMENDED WINES
Colli Albani (Lazio): dry white wine served at 50°F / 10°C
Oltrepò Pavese rosato (Lombardy): rosé served at 50°F / 10°C

1 Peel and slice the turnip, sprinkle with salt and let it sit for 20 minutes, then wash and dry. Clean the savoy cabbage, remove the central core and cut into strips. Scald for an instant in a pot of boiling salted water, drain and set aside. Clean a carrot and peel it, trim the zucchini, clean a stalk of celery, remove the threads and clean the leek. Wash all the vegetables and chop into small pieces. Place in a pan, add the peas, about a quart of water and a bit of washed, minced parsley. Bring it slowly to a boil, salt and cook for 45 minutes.

2 In the meantime, clean and wash the remaining stalk of celery and carrot, wash the remaining parsley and finely mince everything with the garlic and drained, squeezed mushrooms. Scald the tomato in a small saucepan of boiling water, remove the seeds and the vegetable water and mince. Wash the anchovy, remove the bones and mince. Place in a saucepan with the oil and, mixing with a wooden spoon, break it up. Add the minced vegetables and mushrooms and sauté for about 3 minutes over moderate heat. Finally, add the minced tomato and continue cooking over moderate heat for about 5 minutes, stirring occasionally. Add the mixture to the vegetable broth, add the taglierini and cook, then serve the soup piping hot.

PRACTICAL SUGGESTIONS
If you want to make this soup even more tasty and rich, add a few cubes of prosciutto, fried with the minced vegetables and mushrooms. Serve with slices of toasted homemade bread.

Tortelloni with Tofu and Radicchio

INGREDIENTS

serves 4

For the filling

2 lb. – 800 g RED TREVISO RADICCHIO

3 tablespoons SESAME SEED OIL

SALT and PEPPER to taste

1/2 lb. – 200 g TOFU

1 tablespoon LEMON JUICE

3/4 lb. – 300 g FRESH EGG PASTA DOUGH

1 EGG WHITE for brushing

For the seasoning

1/2 lb. – 200 g ZUCCHINI

1 LEEK

3 tablespoons SESAME SEED OIL

10 oz. – 250 g PLUM TOMATOES

EQUIPMENT

2 pots, 2 saucepans, a small saucepan, a mixing bowl

1 blender, a serving dish

Difficulty	**AVERAGE**
Preparation Time	**30 MIN.**
Cooking Time	**30 MIN.**
Method of cooking	**STOVETOP**
Microwave	**NO**
Freezing	**NO**
Keeping Time	**3 DAYS**

SPECIAL NOTE

Tofu, which is similar to a soft, fresh cheese, is obtained from soy curd. It is especially rich in vegetable protein, and has no fats or cholesterol.

RECOMMENDED WINES

Colli di Conegliano bianco (Veneto): dry white wine served at 50°F / 10°C

Elba Ansonica (Tuscany): dry white wine served at 50°F / 10°C

1 Bring salted water to boil in a pot, scald the radicchio for a minute, drain, dry and chop into thin slices. Season in a saucepan with 3 tablespoons oil, salt and pepper, then remove from the heat and cool. Scald the tofu in a small saucepan of lightly salted boiling water, acidulated with the lemon juice. Drain and whip in the blender, adding a few tablespoons cooking water. Place it in a mixing bowl with the radicchio, salt and pepper, and mix until you have a uniform mixture.

2 Roll out the dough to a thin layer and divide into 2.5 inch – 6 centimeter squares. Brush the edges with the beaten egg white, place a bit of prepared filling in the center of each one, and fold the pasta, forming a triangle. Press the edges and again fold the two corners of the widest part, overlapping them and pressing them well.

3 Clean the zucchini and the leek. Wash them, dry them and cut into thin strips. Heat the oil in a saucepan, wilt the leek without browning it, add the zucchini and cook 5-7 minutes. Add the tomatoes, mix and cook 2 minutes. Bring a generous amount of water to boil, salt it, and cook the tortelloni for 5-7 minutes. Drain, transfer to a serving dish and season with the zucchini and tomato sauce. Serve piping hot.

PRACTICAL SUGGESTIONS

If you don't like vegetarian cooking, you can use an equal amount of fresh ricotta in place of the tofu. In this case, you should also use extra virgin olive oil instead of sesame seed oil.

Cauliflower and Zucchini Casserole

INGREDIENTS

serves 4

1 lb. – 500 g ZUCCHINI
2 SHALLOTS
2.2 lb. – 1 kg CAULIFLOWER
1/4 lb. – 60 g BUTTER
SALT and PEPPER to taste
3 oz. – 70 g CHICKEN LIVERS
1 tablespoon EXTRA VIRGIN OLIVE OIL
2/3 lb. – 350 g FRESH EGG PASTA DOUGH

EQUIPMENT

a steam cooker
a vegetable mill, 2 saucepans
a frying pan (preferably cast iron)
a rolling pin
a pot
a bowl
a baking dish

Difficulty	AVERAGE
Preparation Time	30 MIN.
Cooking Time	1 HOUR
Method of cooking	STOVETOP AND OVEN
Microwave	YES
Freezing	YES
Keeping Time	2 DAYS

SPECIAL NOTE

All food oils can be adulterated. The easiest way is to mix high quality with lower quality or "regenerated" oils (old or altered oils that have been rectified through chemical processes).

RECOMMENDED WINES
Barbera del Monferrato (Piedmont): light red wine served at 61°F / 16°C
Lambrusco di Sorbara red (Emilia–Romagna):
light red wine served at 61°F / 16°C

1 Wash the zucchini and cut into strips. Clean the shallots, wash and mince. Wash the cauliflower, break into flowerets and steam cook for 5 minutes. Drain and run through the vegetable mill. In a saucepan with 1/3 the butter, add the zucchini and sauté 4–5 minutes with a pinch of salt and pepper. Cube the chicken livers and sauté in a frying pan until they are browned on all sides.

2 Roll out the dough into thin sheets, cut into rectangles 4.5 by 3 inches (12 by 8 cm) and cook a few at a time in a pot of salted boiling water. Remove as soon as they float to the top, place in a bowl of cold water, drain again and place on a damp dishcloth.

3 Butter a baking dish, place a layer of pasta on it, and add a layer of the cauliflower mixture on top, along with a few cubes of chicken liver and some of the prepared zucchini strips. Continue, alternating the ingredients and ending with the pasta. Brush the top with the remaining butter, place the baking dish in the oven preheated to 350°F, and cook the casserole for 20 minutes. Serve piping hot.

PRACTICAL SUGGESTIONS
As the various ingredients that make up this recipe are already cooked, you don't need to leave the casserole in the oven for too long, only enough to cook the casserole and lightly brown it.

Eggplant Cream with Tortelli

INGREDIENTS

serves 4

1 lb. – 500 g EGGPLANT
2 oz. – 1 bunch BASIL
1 ONION
1 clove GARLIC
5 TOMATOES
half A RED BELL PEPPER
2 tablespoons EXTRA VIRGIN OLIVE OIL
SALT and CAYENNE PEPPER to taste
1/2 quart – 1 generous liter
VEGETABLE BROTH
1 lb. – 400 g ready–made MEATLESS TORTELLI

EQUIPMENT

a skillet
a vegetable mill
a pot

Difficulty	AVERAGE
Preparation Time	15 MIN. + 30 MIN.
Cooking Time	1 HOUR 10 MIN.
Method of cooking	STOVETOP
Microwave	NO
Freezing	NO
Keeping Time	2 DAYS

SPECIAL NOTE

The Italian word *tortello* is a generic term that dates back to the 14th century. It is often used as a synonym for tortellone, and is used to indicate many recipes with a pasta base.

1 Wash the eggplants, trim and chop into cubes. Place in a colander, sprinkle with a little salt and let them sit for about a half hour, so they will loss their bitter vegetable water. Wash the basil and chop it. Peel the onion, wash it and chop it coarsely. Peel the garlic and lightly crush it.

2 Wash the tomatoes, chop them into pieces and remove the seeds and vegetable water. Remove the seeds and white portion of the bell pepper, wash it and mince it. Wilt the onion and garlic in a skillet with the oil, without browning them. Add the drained, dried eggplants, the tomatoes, the pepper, the basil and salt and pepper.

3 Continue cooking for about 15 minutes over moderate heat, stirring occasionally with a wooden spoon. Pour in the broth, bring to a boil and continue cooking over low heat for 35–40 minutes.

4 Run the mixture through a vegetable mill and place in a cooking skillet. Cook the tortelli in a pot of salted boiling water, drain when al dente, add to the vegetable puree and cook together for a few minutes. Serve immediately.

PRACTICAL SUGGESTIONS

Eggplants should be firm and compact. When you rap on them with a finger, they should sound hollow. Choose those with an oblong form, as they generally have a compact flesh and few seeds.

Steamed Ravioli

Valle d'Aosta bianco (Valle d'Aosta): dry white wine served at 50°F / 10°C
Castel del Monte bianco (Puglia): dry white wine served at 50°F / 10°C

1 Prepare the pasta, mixing the eggs, lukewarm water and salt with the flour. Knead the dough with your hands until you have eliminated all lumps, then let it rest 30 minutes, wrapped in a dishtowel.

2 In the meantime, remove the harder ribs from the cabbage leaves and boil the leaves with the cod in a pot of salted water, to which you have added the stalk of celery and the peeled onion. When done, drain the cod and cabbage leaves (setting the cooking liquid aside). Chop them coarsely, transfer them to a mixing bowl and season with the sour cream and a pinch of salt.

3 Take out the pasta and roll into a sheet about 1/32 inch – 1 mm thick, then cut out squares 3–3.5 inches – 8–9 centimeters in size and place a spoonful of the prepared filling in the center of each one. Wrap the pasta around the filling without sealing the ravioli completely, then steam cook for 20–25 minutes, reusing the cod cooking broth. Arrange the ravioli on a serving dish and serve.

PRACTICAL SUGGESTIONS

If you want to prepare sour cream yourself, place 1/4 lb. – 100 g whipping cream in a jar, add a teaspoon lemon juice, shake and let it sit in the refrigerator for 30 minutes.

INGREDIENTS

serves 4

For the pasta

2 EGGS

SALT to taste

1 lb. – 400 g FLOUR

For the filling

1 – 1 1/3 lb. – 400–500 g SAVOY CABBAGE

1 lb. – 400 g COD

SALT to taste

1 stalk CELERY

1 ONION

1/2 cup SOUR CREAM or sweet cream

EQUIPMENT

a pot, a mixing bowl

a steam cooker

a serving dish

Difficulty	**AVERAGE**
Preparation Time	**30 MIN. + 30 MIN.**
Cooking Time	**45 MIN.**
Method of cooking	**STOVETOP**
Microwave	**NO**
Freezing	**YES**
Keeping Time	**3 DAYS**

SPECIAL NOTE

Cod became quite popular in Europe around 1300, when commercial trade began to develop and markets started selling a variety of commodities.

Herb Tortelli alla Lombarda

INGREDIENTS
serves 4

I 3/4 cup – 200 g WHITE FLOUR
I EGG, I packet SAFFRON, a pinch SALT
For the filling
I 3/4 lb. – 700 g SWISS CHARD
SALT and PEPPER to taste
1/4 lb. – 100 g RICOTTA,
3 tablespoons GRATED PARMESAN
I EGG, I sprig THYME, I sprig MARJORAM
I pinch POWDERED CINNAMON
NUTMEG to taste, POWDERED CLOVES to taste
I pinch SAFFRON
For the seasoning
1/4 cup – 40 g BUTTER
2 tablespoons GRATED PARMESAN
I pinch POWDERED CINNAMON
I pinch minced THYME and MARJORAM

EQUIPMENT
2 pots, a food processor, a bowl, a small saucepan

Difficulty	AVERAGE
Preparation Time	30 MIN. + 30 MIN.
Cooking Time	15 MIN.
Method of cooking	STOVETOP
Microwave	NO
Freezing	YES
Keeping Time	3 DAYS

SPECIAL NOTE
Thyme *(Thymus vulgaris)* is an essential herb in much of western cooking. It is a basic component of *bouquet garni* and many *court–bouillons*.

RECOMMENDED WINES
Garda Bresciano chiaretto (Lombardy): rosé served at 50°F / 10°C
Bosco Eliceo Sauvignon (Emilia Romagna):
mellow, aromatic white wine served at 50°F / 10°C

I Prepare the pasta. Sift the flour, place an egg, the salt and the saffron, dissolved in 4–5 tablespoons lukewarm water, in the center. Work until you obtain a smooth, silky dough, then wrap in a cloth and let it rest 30 minutes. In the meantime, prepare the filling. Wash the chard and remove the stalks, cook for 4 minutes in a pot of salted boiling water, drain, squeeze and put through the food processor. Place in a bowl, add the ricotta, the parmesan, the egg, the finely minced thyme and marjoram, the cinnamon, a pinch of nutmeg and a pinch of cloves, the saffron dissolved in a half tablespoon water, salt and pepper. Mix everything with a wooden spoon until you have a uniform mixture.

2 Roll out the dough very thin, and using a toothed pastry wheel, cut it into rectangles about 3.5 by 2 inches – 7 by 5 cm. Brush the edges with water, place a half tablespoon of the herb mixture in the center, and wrap up the pasta like a candy. Press on the edges to seal.

3 Cook the tortelli for 5–7 minutes in a large pot of salted boiling water. In the meantime, melt the butter in a small saucepan. Drain the tortelli and season them with the melted butter, the grated parmesan, a pinch of cinnamon, a bit of minced thyme and marjoram, and serve immediately.

PRACTICAL SUGGESTIONS
If necessary, you can prepare these tortelli a day in advance, but be sure to leave them on a flat surface between two layers of cloth. You can use a pasta machine to speed up pasta preparation time.

Spaghettoni Salad

INGREDIENTS

serves 4

1 lb. – 400 g SPAGHETTONI (thick spaghetti)
SALT to taste
3 tablespoons EXTRA VIRGIN OLIVE OIL
1 stalk CELERY
1 sprig PARSLEY
1 sprig BASIL
2 TOMATOES
1 YELLOW BELL PEPPER
1 GREEN BELL PEPPER
a dozen GREEN OLIVES
1 tablespoon CAPERS IN SALT
1/3 lb. – 120 g FONTINA CHEESE
1 teaspoon LEMON JUICE
1 teaspoon MUSTARD

EQUIPMENT

a pot, a small bowl
a serving bowl

Difficulty	EASY
Preparation Time	30 MIN.
Cooking Time	20 MIN.
Method of cooking	STOVETOP
Microwave	NO
Freezing	NO
Keeping Time	1 DAY

SPECIAL NOTE

The two most common types of mustard are Dijon and English. Use of mustard as a condiment comes from the French, who began producing it in 1390.

RECOMMENDED WINES
Oltrepò Pavese Chardonnay (Lombardy):
mellow, aromatic white wine served at 50°F / 10°C
Verdicchio di Matelica (Marche): dry white wine served at 50°F / 10°C

1 Boil the spaghettoni in a large pot of salted boiling water. Drain when al dente, place on a flat surface, season with 2–3 tablespoons oil and cool completely. If necessary, add a bit more oil to prevent them from sticking together.

2 Wash and dry the celery, parsley and basil. Cut the tomatoes halfway open, remove the seeds, salt them and let them drain upside down. Remove the seeds and white parts of the peppers. Pit the olives, and rinse and dry the capers.

3 Using a sharp knife, coarsely chop the fontina and all prepared ingredients, then mix with the pasta in a deep serving bowl.

4 In a small bowl, dilute the lemon juice with the mustard and a pinch of cayenne pepper (a little more or less, depending on your taste). Beat well with a fork until you obtain a uniform sauce. Season everything and serve immediately.

PRACTICAL SUGGESTIONS
You can also add boiled, diced carrots, zucchini and other ingredients to the vegetables. You can use diced mozzarella instead of the fontina.

Fusilli with Spinach and Pine Nuts

INGREDIENTS

serves 4

1 lb. – 450 g FROZEN SPINACH
SALT and PEPPER to taste
2 STRIPS GREEN PEPPER IN OIL
1 sprig MINCED PARSLEY
1/2 lb. – 200 g PIEDMONT RICOTTA
MILK as necessary
3/4 lb. – 350 g SHORT FUSILLI (a
corkscrew–shaped pasta)
1 clove GARLIC
1/8 cup – 30 g BUTTER
handful PINE NUTS
GRATED PARMESAN to taste

EQUIPMENT

2 pots
a mixing bowl
a saucepan
a deep Pyrex dish

Difficulty	AVERAGE
Preparation Time	30 MIN.
Cooking Time	30 MIN.
Method of cooking	STOVETOP
Microwave	NO
Freezing	NO
Keeping Time	1 DAY

SPECIAL NOTE

Piedmont ricotta, locally known as *seirass* (from the Latin *serum*), is shaped into a pointed cone form, making it easy to distinguish from other types of ricotta.

RECOMMENDED WINES
Collio goriziano Sauvignon (Friuli–Venezia Giulia):
mellow, aromatic white wine served at 50°F / 10°C
Lambrusco reggiano (Emilia–Romagna): rosé served at 57°F / 14°C

1 Defrost the spinach in a pot with a small amount of salted boiling water. Drain, squeeze, chop coarsely and set aside. Cut the drained pepper strips into cubes. Mix the pepper cubes and parsley with the ricotta in a mixing bowl. Dilute with 2–3 tablespoons milk to obtain a soft cream. Boil the pasta in a pot with a generous amount of salted water.

2 In the meantime, brown the garlic clove in a saucepan with the butter. Remove the garlic, add the spinach and let it season, then add the pine nuts and a pinch of freshly ground pepper. Cook for a few minutes, then remove from the heat.

3 Drain the pasta somewhat, season with the ricotta cream and place in a Pyrex dish. Sprinkle the surface with grated parmesan and serve immediately.

PRACTICAL SUGGESTIONS
When preparing these fusilli, you can use small, dark green salad leaves instead of spinach, or even nettles, if you can find them. You can use a fresh pepper instead of the preserved one; blacken it in the gas flame or the oven, place in a paper sack for 10 minutes and then peel.

Aromatic Tortelli with Mascarpone

INGREDIENTS
serves 4

For the filling
1/3 lb. – 150 g SPINACH
1/3 lb. – 150 g SWISS CHARD
1 oz. – 20 g BUTTER
1/2 lb. – 200 g ROMAN RICOTTA
1/4 lb. – 100 g MASCARPONE, 1 EGG
1 tablespoon GRATED PARMESAN
1 sprig THYME, 1 sprig MARJORAM
1 pinch NUTMEG, SALT and PEPPER to taste
3/4 LB. – 300 G FRESH EGG PASTA DOUGH

For the seasoning
1/4 cup – 50 g BUTTER, 3–4 SAGE leaves
2 tablespoons GRATED PARMESAN

EQUIPMENT
a frying pan, a food processor, a mixing bowl
a toothed pastry wheel, a pot
a small saucepan, a serving dish

Difficulty	AVERAGE
Preparation Time	50 MIN.
Cooking Time	10 MIN.
Method of cooking	STOVETOP
Microwave	NO
Freezing	NO
Keeping Time	3 DAYS

SPECIAL NOTE
You can make a stimulating tea with the leaves
of thyme, heather, blackberry, bilberry and
speedwell. It is known as "moor tea."

RECOMMENDED WINES
Cortese dell'Alto Monferrato (Piedmont):
mellow, aromatic white wine served at 50°F / 10°C
Biferno bianco (Molise): dry white wine served at 50°F / 10°C

1 Clean the spinach and chard, wash, cut into strips, place in a frying pan with the butter and sauté for 5 minutes. Run through a food processor and, if necessary, dry it out a bit in the frying pan. Place in a bowl, add the ricotta and mascarpone and mix well.

2 Add the egg, the grated cheese, the finely minced thyme and marjoram, the nutmeg and a pinch of salt and freshly ground pepper to the mixture. Mix the ingredients with a wooden spoon to blend well.

3 Roll out the egg dough into a very thin layer, and using a toothed pastry wheel, cut it into squares about 1.5 inches – 4 centimeters in size. Brush the edges with water, place a bit of the prepared mixture in the center and fold into a triangle shape, pressing the edges with your fingers. Cook the tortelli in a large pot of boiling salted water for 5–7 minutes.

4 In the meantime, melt the butter with the sage in a small saucepan, drain the tortelli when al dente, place in the serving dish, drizzle with the melted butter and sage, sprinkle with grated parmesan and serve piping hot.

PRACTICAL SUGGESTIONS
If you want a more flavorful filling, before adding the chard and spinach, sauté a minced onion, a tablespoon minced parsley and a whole clove of garlic in the butter. Remove the garlic before adding the vegetables.

Vegetable Minestrone with Tortellini

INGREDIENTS

serves 4

1.5 oz. – 30 g PLAIN, UNSMOKED BACON
I clove GARLIC
EXTRA VIRGIN OLIVE OIL as necessary
1/2 quart – I liter BROTH
I small package FROZEN SOUP VEGETABLES
I CAN CANNELLINI BEANS
1/4 lb. – 100 g TORTELLINI
SALT and PEPPER to taste
I sprig PARSLEY

EQUIPMENT

a chopping knife
a skillet
a soup tureen

Difficulty	AVERAGE
Preparation Time	20 MIN.
Cooking Time	50 MIN.
Method of cooking	STOVETOP
Microwave	NO
Freezing	NO
Keeping Time	I DAY

SPECIAL NOTE

While parsley is used as often as salt in continental Europe, in the Anglo–Saxon world it is also considered an ornamental plant, especially the variety *crispum.*

RECOMMENDED WINES

Colline Novarese Croatina (Piedmont): light red wine served at 61°F / 16°C
Colli Berici Merlot (Veneto): light red wine served at 61°F / 16°C

I Using a chopping knife, mince the bacon with the clove of garlic, from which you have removed the green shoot in the center. Wilt the minced mixture in a skillet with a tablespoon oil. Pour in the broth, bring to a boil and add the frozen vegetables.

2 Cover and cook for 30 minutes over moderate heat, then drain the cannellini beans, wash under running water, and add. Add the tortellini after 10 minutes, adjust the salt and finish cooking.

3 In the meantime, trim, wash and dry the parsley, add it to the minestrone and pour it immediately into a soup tureen. Complete with a grind of pepper and a drizzle of raw oil, then serve.

PRACTICAL SUGGESTIONS

For this recipe to be successful, you should use beef and capon or beef and chicken broth, but if you want to make it lighter, you can use vegetable broth and add minced onion, carrot and garlic instead of bacon.

Rice with Croquettes

INGREDIENTS

serves 4

For the croquettes

3/4 lb. – 350 g COD FILLETS
1/2 lb. – 250 g POTATOES
SALT and PEPPER to taste, 1 ONION
1 tablespoon EXTRA VIRGIN OLIVE OIL
1 EGG, 1 EGG YOLK
1 tablespoon WHITE FLOUR
PEANUT OIL FOR FRYING

2 oz. – 50 g SULTANA RAISINS
3/4 lb. – 350 g RICE, SALT to taste
2 oz. – 40 g SLIVERED ALMONDS
1 oz. – 20 g BUTTER

EQUIPMENT

a bowl, a pot, a cast iron saucepan
a cup, a saucepan, a frying pan
a serving dish

Difficulty	**AVERAGE**
Preparation Time	**30 MIN.**
Cooking Time	**1 HOUR 10 MIN.**
Method of cooking	**STOVETOP**
Microwave	**NO**
Freezing	**NO**
Keeping Time	**1 DAY**

SPECIAL NOTE

Cultivated for millennia in China, India and
Indochina, rice arrived in Italy when the Arabs
reached Spain and Sicily. From Spain, it was
imported to Lombardy and Piedmont.

RECOMMENDED WINES
Langhe bianco (Piedmont): dry white wine served at 50°F / 10°C
Soave (Veneto): dry white wine served at 50°F / 10°C

1 Prepare the croquettes. Wash the cod fillets, dry with a dishtowel, mince and place in a bowl. Wash the potatoes and cook in a pot with a generous amount of salted water until tender. Drain, peel, put through the potato ricer, allow to cool and add to the minced cod fillets.

2 Peel the onion, wash and mince it finely. Place it in a non–stick saucepan with the oil and wilt it without browning it. Add it to the fish and potato mixture, add the whole egg, the egg yolk, a pinch of salt and pepper, and mix with a wooden spoon until the ingredients are well–blended. Using your hands, form cherry–sized croquettes and fry in abundant hot but not boiling oil, then place on absorbent paper towels.

3 Soften the raisins in a cup with a bit of lukewarm water. Cook the rice in abundant boiling salted water and drain when al dente. In the meantime, sauté the almonds and raisins (drained and dried) in a saucepan with butter, stirring often, then add the rice and season for a few minutes. Place it in a serving dish, pressing lightly with the back of a spoon to form a small cavity, and fill it with the croquettes. Serve hot.

PRACTICAL SUGGESTIONS
Before boiling the rice, be sure there are no impurities among the grains, then sprinkle it into a pot in which you have brought at least 1 quart of lightly salted water to a boil.

Rice with Eggs

RECOMMENDED WINES
Oltrepò Pavese Bonarda (Lombardy): light red wine served at 61°F / 16°C
Parrina rosso (Tuscany): light red wine served at 61°F / 16°C

1 Heat a generous amount of salted water in a pot. When it comes to a boil, sprinkle in the rice, and boil it al dente. Drain well, pour into the mold and keep warm..

2 Blacken the pepper over the gas flame or in the oven, then peel it, remove the seeds and cut into strips. Melt 1 oz. – 20 grams butter in a saucepan, and sauté the green pepper slices with a pinch of salt and freshly ground pepper over moderate heat. Add the tomato sauce, mix well with a wooden spoon to blend the ingredients, and cook over low heat for about 10 minutes. Remove the saucepan from the heat and keep the sauce warm.

3 Place the remaining butter in another saucepan, heat it and cook the eggs sunny side up. Turn the rice out of the mold onto a serving dish. Place the prepared eggs on it in a circle, then pour the tomato sauce and green pepper in the center of the ring and serve immediately.

PRACTICAL SUGGESTIONS
To successfully make eggs sunny side up, break the eggs into a plate, and when the butter begins to foam, let them slide in delicately. Cook over high heat for 4 minutes, so the white hardens quickly.

INGREDIENTS
serves 4

1/2 lb. – 200 g RICE
1 GREEN PEPPER
1/4 cup – 50 g BUTTER
SALT and PEPPER to taste
3/4 lb. – 300 g TOMATO SAUCE
4 tablespoons EXTRA VIRGIN OLIVE OIL
4 EGGS

EQUIPMENT
a pot
a mold with a hole in the middle
2 saucepans
a serving dish

Difficulty	AVERAGE
Preparation Time	15 MIN.
Cooking Time	30 MIN.
Method of cooking	STOVETOP
Microwave	NO
Freezing	NO
Keeping Time	1 DAY

SPECIAL NOTE
In the fourteenth century, eggs were cooked in ways that gradually fell into disuse: under the coals, grilled, or scrambled, sweetened and spiced as a filling for fried ravioli.

Rice and Zucchini Mold

INGREDIENTS

serves 4

1 lb. – 400 g ZUCCHINI
1 clove GARLIC
3 tablespoons EXTRA VIRGIN OLIVE OIL
SALT and PEPPER to taste
3/4 lb. – 300 g SUPERFINE RICE
1/4 cup – 50 g BUTTER
3 tablespoons GRATED PARMESAN
1/4 lb. – 100 g EMMENTAL CHEESE
1 tablespoon BREAD CRUMBS

EQUIPMENT

a saucepan
a pot
a baking dish

Difficulty	AVERAGE
Preparation Time	15 MIN.
Cooking Time	35 MIN.
Method of cooking	STOVETOP
Microwave	YES
Freezing	NO
Keeping Time	3 DAYS

SPECIAL NOTE

Emmental is a pressed, cooked cheese that is rich in fat. It is produced in Switzerland, French Savoy and Bavaria. Melted Emmental is used to make cheese spreads.

RECOMMENDED WINES
Frascati Superiore (Lazio): dry white wine served at 50°F / 10°C
Verdicchio di Matelica (Marche): dry white wine served at 50°F / 10°C

1 Trim the zucchini, wash and cut into rounds. Peel the garlic, place in a saucepan with the oil and wilt. Add the zucchini and sauté briefly, mixing with a wooden spoon. Add salt and pepper and lightly brown on both sides.

2 In the meantime, boil the rice for about 10 minutes in a pot of boiling salted water. Drain and season with a little less than half (20 grams) the butter, and the grated cheese. As the rice is cooking, cut the Emmental into thin slices.

3 Lightly butter a baking dish, add a layer of rice and then make a layer of zucchini and some sliced Emmental. Alternate the rice with the zucchini and cheese until the ingredients are finished. End with the rice and a few slices of Emmental, and dot with the remaining butter.

4 Sprinkle the mold with the bread crumbs and place in a preheated 375°F oven for about 15 minutes, until the surface is lightly browned. Serve hot in the baking dish.

PRACTICAL SUGGESTIONS
When you put the baking dish in the oven, you should cover it with a sheet of aluminum foil. Remove the foil after 10 minutes to allow the surface to brown lightly.

Sicilian Risotto

INGREDIENTS

serves 4

SALT and PEPPER to taste
scant 1 lb. – 360 g RICE
1 ONION
3 tablespoons EXTRA VIRGIN OLIVE OIL
1 tablespoon APPLE CIDER VINEGAR
1 tablespoon ANCHOVY PASTE
1 cup DRY WHITE WINE
2 rather large TOMATOES
2 tablespoons PITTED BLACK OLIVES
OREGANO to taste

EQUIPMENT

a pot, a small saucepan
a frying pan, a mixing bowl
absorbent paper towels
a serving dish

Difficulty	AVERAGE
Preparation Time	25 MIN.
Cooking Time	35 MIN.
Method of cooking	STOVETOP
Microwave	NO
Freezing	NO
Keeping Time	3 DAYS

SPECIAL NOTE

Rice has absolutely no fats, and is thus good for anyone who needs to keep their cholesterol level down. Its low sodium content also makes it suitable for anyone with high blood pressure.

RECOMMENDED WINES
Colli Euganei Merlot (Veneto): light red wine served at 61°F / 16°C
Colli piacentini Pinot nero (Emilia–Romagna):
light red wine served at 64°F / 18°C

1 Bring a generous amount of salted water to boil in a pot. When it begins to boil, add the rice and cook al dente. In the meantime, peel the onion, mince and sauté in a small saucepan with the extra virgin olive oil. When it is golden, add the vinegar and anchovy paste, mix well with a wooden spoon, add pepper and pour in the wine. Season 5–6 minutes, the remove from the heat.

2 Wash and dry the tomatoes, then cut them into medium sized wedges, which you should squeeze slightly to remove the seeds and vegetable water. Pour a generous amount of oil into a frying pan or a fryer, if you prefer. Add the tomatoes when it is very hot. Fry 2–3 minutes on each side, remove with a slotted spoon and place on absorbent paper towels to remove any excess oil.

3 When the rice is cooked al dente, drain it and place it in a mixing bowl. Add the fried tomatoes, pitted olives, a pinch of oregano, and the anchovy paste, and mix to blend the ingredients well. Transfer to a serving dish and serve warm or cold, as you prefer.

PRACTICAL SUGGESTIONS
To make this dish more flavorful, you can boil the rice in 2/3 quart vegetable broth rather than water. The rice should cook in a wide, shallow skillet that allows a uniform distribution of heat

Rice with Onions and Cheese

INGREDIENTS

serves 4

3/4 lb. – 300 g SUPERFINE ARBORIO RICE
1 3/4 lb. – 700 g ONIONS
2 OZ. – 1 bunch PARSLEY
1/4 cup – 50 g BUTTER
2 tablespoons DRY WHITE WINE
3 tablespoons – 1 dl CREAM
SALT and PEPPER to taste
3 tablespoons – 60 g GRATED PARMESAN
1 pinch PAPRIKA

EQUIPMENT

a pot
a saucepan
a baking dish

Difficulty	AVERAGE
Preparation Time	20 MIN.
Cooking Time	1 HOUR
Method of cooking	STOVETOP AND OVEN
Microwave	YES
Freezing	NO
Keeping Time	2 DAYS

SPECIAL NOTE

For a cough and cold, prepare a decoction of 1/2 ounce – 10 grams onion per cup of water or milk; drink a cup in the morning and evening.

RECOMMENDED WINES
Riviera Ligure di Ponente Pigato (Liguria):
dry white wine served at 50°F / 10°C
Gioia del Colle rosato (Puglia): rosé served at 54°F / 12°C

❖

1 Place a generous amount of water in a pot and bring to a boil. Add the rice, cook 5 minutes and drain. Peel the onions, wash and mince them coarsely, and carefully wash the parsley, and mince.

2 Melt 1/8 cup – 30 grams butter in a saucepan, add the onions and wilt them without browning. Add the wine and 3 tablespoons water and continue cooking for about 20 minutes, stirring occasionally with a wooden spoon.

3 Add the cream, rice and parsley, a pinch of salt and freshly ground pepper, and mix with a wooden spoon to blend all the ingredients well. Remove the mixture from the heat, add the grated cheese, mix and pour the rice into a buttered baking dish.

4 Sprinkle the rice with paprika and bake in a preheated 350°F oven for about 30 minutes, until the surface is lightly browned. Serve hot in the baking dish.

PRACTICAL SUGGESTIONS
If you want to lighten the onion flavor, slice and soak in cold water for a few hours. To soften the flavor even more, soak the onions in milk, then drain, dry and proceed as indicated.

Exotic Paella

INGREDIENTS

serves 4–6

I CHICKEN, about 2 lb. – I kilo
I tablespoon WHITE FLOUR
5 tablespoons EXTRA VIRGIN OLIVE OIL
2 ONIONS
I BELL PEPPER, cut into julienne strips
1/3 lb. – 150 g SHELLED PEAS (or frozen)
1/3 lb. – 150 g PLUM TOMATOES
I CLOVE
half A FRESH HOT PEPPER, chopped
SALT and PEPPER to taste
1/8 cup – 30 g BUTTER
3/4 lb. – 300 g RICE
I packet SAFFRON
2 cups – half a liter BROTH

EQUIPMENT

a saucepan, a terra–cotta saucepan

Difficulty	AVERAGE
Preparation Time	30 MIN.
Cooking Time	I HOUR 20 MIN.
Method of cooking	STOVETOP AND OVEN
Microwave	YES
Freezing	NO
Keeping Time	2 DAYS

SPECIAL NOTE

Paella is considered the emblem of Spanish cooking. The most well–known version is *paella valenciana*, but the success of this dish, especially with foreigners, has led to many variations.

I Clean, singe and wash the chicken, cut into pieces and lightly flour. Place it in a saucepan with 2 tablespoons oil and brown for 15 minutes, turning often, then remove from the pan and keep warm.

2 Add the rest of the oil to the pan and sauté the finely minced onions, the bell pepper, the peas, the tomatoes broken up with a fork, the clove and the hot pepper. Salt and let it cook slowly for about 20 minutes.

3 Place the butter in a terra–cotta saucepan with the chicken and cook slowly, covered, for 20 minutes, turning often. Add the rice to the chicken and let it sauté well, as for a normal risotto, then add the saffron dissolved in a small amount of broth.

4 After 5 or 6 minutes, add the broth and prepared vegetables to the rice and place the saucepan in a preheated 350°F oven for about 15 minutes. Serve the paella piping hot in the baking dish.

PRACTICAL SUGGESTIONS
Regional Spanish cuisine has inherited many baked rice recipes from the period of Arab domination, but each one uses only certain ingredients (fish, shellfish, meat, or vegetables). Only with paella can the cook combine everything he wants to add.

Risotto with Tench

INGREDIENTS

serves 4

1 lb. – 400 g TENCH

1.5 oz. – 30 g PARSLEY

1 small stalk CELERY

1 sprig BASIL

1 CARROT

1 small ONION

2 cloves GARLIC

5 tablespoons EXTRA VIRGIN OLIVE OIL

3 tablespoons DRY WHITE WINE

1 tablespoon TOMATO PASTE

SALT and PEPPER to taste

scant lb. – 350 g RICE

4 tablespoons GRATED PARMESAN

EQUIPMENT

a skillet

a mixing bowl

a saucepan

Difficulty	AVERAGE
Preparation Time	20 MIN.
Cooking Time	1 HOUR
Method of cooking	STOVETOP
Microwave	YES
Freezing	NO
Keeping Time	2 DAYS

SPECIAL NOTE

Like paper, tench was once considered a "secondary product" in fish farms in freshwater bodies of water like rice fields.

RECOMMENDED WINES

Valcalepio bianco (Lombardy): dry white wine served at 50°F / 10°C
Verdicchio dei Castelli di Jesi (Marche): mellow, aromatic white wine served at 50°F / 10°C

1 Throw the tench into boiling water, then drain, scale, clean well, wash and chop into pieces (without discarding the head). Wash and mince the parsley, celery, basil, carrot, onion and garlic.

2 Place the mixture in a skillet with 2 tablespoons oil and place the pan on the heat. Sauté a few minutes, and then add the pieces of fish, moisten with 3 tablespoons white wine, mix and sauté for 5 more minutes, stirring occasionally.

3 Add the tomato paste dissolved in a half a cup of hot water, add salt and pepper and cook for about 20 minutes, covered, stirring occasionally. Then puree everything and place in a mixing bowl.

4 Place 3 tablespoons oil in a saucepan, heat, then add the rice and toast it a few minutes. Then add the prepared puree and cook the rice for 15–18 minutes, adding a few spoonfuls hot water or broth during cooking and adjusting the salt when done. Before serving, blend in the grated parmesan and a pinch of freshly ground pepper.

PRACTICAL SUGGESTIONS

For a better presentation of the risotto, we recommend buying a little extra fish. Before pureeing the sauce, select the four best pieces of fish and set them aside. When cooking is complete, arrange them on the risotto, sprinkle with a pinch of minced parsley and serve.

Rice Pilaf with Curry

INGREDIENTS

serves 4

For the rice pilaf

1/4 cup — 40 g BUTTER

half an ONION, sliced

1 CARROT, minced, 1 stalk CELERY, chopped

3 CLOVES, 1 lb. — 400 g CARNAROLI RICE

2 1/4 cups — scant 3/4 liter HOT BROTH

For the seasoning

3 oz. — 150 g RED BELL PEPPER

1 GREEN APPLE

6 oz. — 150 g SHELLED PEAS (can be frozen)

3 tablespoons EXTRA VIRGIN OLIVE OIL

2/3 lb. — 250 g CHICKEN BREASTS, diced

half an ONION, 1 tablespoon CURRY

SALT and PEPPER to taste

3 tablespoons CREAM

EQUIPMENT

a skillet, a vegetable mill, a pot

a serving dish

Difficulty	AVERAGE
Preparation Time	20 MIN.
Cooking Time	1 HOUR 10 MIN.
Method of cooking	STOVETOP AND OVEN
Microwave	YES
Freezing	NO
Keeping Time	1 DAY

SPECIAL NOTE

Curry is a mixture of spices in powdered or paste form that is Indian in origin. It consists of coriander, ginger, saffron, cloves, pepper, cardamom, nutmeg and hot peppers.

RECOMMENDED WINES

Boca (Piedmont): medium–bodied red wine served at 64°F / 18°C

Bolgheri Sassicaia (Tuscany): medium–bodied red wine served at 64°F / 18°C

1 Prepare the rice pilaf. Place 1/8 cup – 30 g butter in a saucepan and wilt the onion. Add the carrot, celery and cloves. Let it season 4 minutes, then add the rice and sauté for 2 minutes. Add the broth, cover, and place in a preheated 375°F oven for 20 minutes. When done, remove from the oven, add the remaining butter and mix to separate the rice grains.

2 Clean the bell pepper, wash and dice. Peel the apple and cut into cubes. Heat the peas in a pan with boiling water for 2 minutes, drain and set aside. Heat the oil in a frying pan, add the chicken cubes and brown on all sides, then drain and set aside. Wilt the onion in the same frying pan. Add the apple cubes and let them sauté 3–4 minutes. Add the curry and toast it. Moisten with a small ladle of water, add salt and pepper and cook about 10 minutes. When cooking is completed, whip the apple and onion and add the cream.

3 Place the mixture over the heat again. Add the chicken, the peas, and the bell pepper, and cook 7–8 minutes, mixing often so the sauce does not stick to the bottom. Pressing firmly, place the rice in small buttered molds and unmold on a serving dish. Serve warm accompanied with the prepared curry sauce.

PRACTICAL SUGGESTIONS

If you don't have molds, you can place the rice pilaf in a flat Jell–O mold with a hole in the middle, inside of which you can pour the curry sauce.

Risotto alla Pavese

*Oltrepò Pavese rosso riserva (Lombardy):
light red wine served at 64°F / 18°C
Carmignano rosato (Tuscany): rosé served at 54°F / 12°C*

1 Peel the onion and wash it. Shell the beans and wash. Peel the carrot. Remove the threads from the celery. Wash the carrot and celery and place in a pan with the beans and half an onion. Just cover with cold water, add the peeled garlic, bring to a boil and cook over moderate heat (salting when half done) for about an hour.

2 In the meantime, scald the tomatoes in boiling water for one minute. Drain, remove the skin, seeds and vegetable water, then put through the vegetable mill. Heat the broth in a skillet.

3 Finely mince the remaining onion, place it in a saucepan with the oil and 1 oz. – 20 grams butter, and wilt over low heat without letting it brown. Add the tomato puree and cook over high heat for 5 minutes. Add the drained beans and season briefly.

4 Add the rice and toast it, mixing with a wooden spoon. Add the wine and allow it to evaporate over high heat. Add the hot broth a little at a time and continue cooking 15–18 minutes. Remove the al dente risotto and a little remaining liquid from the heat, thicken with the remaining butter and grated parmesan. Pour onto a hot serving dish and serve immediately.

PRACTICAL SUGGESTIONS
If you're not skilled at making risotto, we recommend using parboiled rice, as even if you make a mistake, it won't overcook or become sticky.

INGREDIENTS
serves 4–6

1 ONION
1 lb. – 500 g BORLOTTI BEANS
1 CARROT
1 stalk CELERY
half a clove GARLIC
SALT to taste
2 firm, ripe TOMATOES
or canned plum tomatoes
1 tablespoon EXTRA VIRGIN OLIVE OIL
1/4 cup – 40 g BUTTER
3/4 lb. – 350 g SUPERFINE ARBORIO RICE
5 tablespoons DRY WHITE WINE
2 1/4 cups – 3/4 liter VEGETABLE BROTH
2 tablespoons GRATED PARMESAN

EQUIPMENT
a pot, a vegetable mill, a skillet
a saucepan, a serving dish

Difficulty	**AVERAGE**
Preparation Time	**15 MIN.**
Cooking Time	**1 HOUR 40 MIN.**
Method of cooking	**STOVETOP**
Microwave	**NO**
Freezing	**NO**
Keeping Time	**1 DAY**

SPECIAL NOTE
Cultivated since ancient times in many regions of Italy, beans were considered peasant food. The oldest species have now been replaced by American varieties.

Dried Salted Cod in Zimino Sauce p48

Cod with Curry p49

Pork with Apples p50

Cacciucco alla Livornese p52

Cima alla Genovese p54

Roast Pork in Water p56

Pitaggio p58

Florentine Meat Loaf p60

Mixed Grilled Meats p61

Spinach Meat Loaf p62

Boiled Meat with Vegetables p64

Roast with Sage p66

Tapulone p68

Mutton Spiedini p70

Freshwater Fish Tegamaccio   p72

Dried Cod in Potacchio   p73

Hake with Herbs   p74

Sole Kebabs   p76

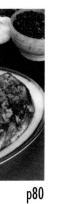

Bass with Fennel   p78

Stewed Sturgeon   p80

Trout Salad   p82

Galician Pescado   p84

Trapani-Style Couscous   p85

Meat and Fish

Dried Salted Cod in Zimino Sauce

INGREDIENTS

serves 4

1 lb. – 400 g FILLETS DRIED SALTED COD
4 cups – 1 liter MILK
2 lb. – 800 g SWISS CHARD
2 cloves GARLIC
1 sprig PARSLEY
2 tablespoons EXTRA VIRGIN OLIVE OIL
SALT and PEPPER to taste
OLIVE OIL FOR FRYING

EQUIPMENT

2 containers for soaking the cod
a pot
a frying pan
absorbent paper towels
a baking dish

Difficulty	**AVERAGE**
Preparation Time	**20 MIN. + 26 HOURS**
Cooking Time	**40 MIN.**
Method of cooking	**STOVETOP AND OVEN**
Microwave	**YES**
Freezing	**NO**
Keeping Time	**2 DAYS**

SPECIAL NOTE

Zimino (also known as *zemin*) is a typical sauce
in Ligurian cuisine, and is used to flavor fish
(dried salted cod, cuttlefish, squid) and crow. The
name comes from the Arabic *assaminu*,
or fatty sauce.

RECOMMENDED WINES
Bianco di Custoza (Veneto): dry white wine served at 50°F / 10°C
Marino (Lazio): dry white wine served at 50°F / 10°C

1 Soak the cod in a container under a thin stream of running water, or change the water often, for 24 hours. Then drain it and place in another container with the milk and soak two more hours. In the meantime, prepare the cooking sauce: trim the chard, wash it and boil it in a pot with only the water remaining after washing it, for about 20 minutes.

2 Peel the garlic, mince it with the trimmed, washed parsley, and add the minced mixture to the boiled vegetables almost at the end of cooking, adding the extra virgin olive oil and a pinch of salt as well. Mix and complete cooking over low heat, being sure that the oil does not fry.

3 When the cod has soaked as indicated, drain it from the milk and fry in a pan with abundant hot olive oil. When it has become golden brown, remove it with a slotted spatula and place it on absorbent paper towels to eliminate excess oil.

4 Place half the vegetables in a baking dish, place the fried cod on top and cover it with the remaining vegetables, then bake about 10 minutes in a preheated 400°F oven, being sure that the vegetables do not dry out too much. Serve hot.

PRACTICAL SUGGESTIONS
To complete this meal, you can add a side dish of boiled potatoes or white rice. The recipe will be just as good if you use fresh cod instead of the fried and salted variety, and you will avoid having to soak it.

Cod with Curry

Lison Pramaggiore Sauvignon (Veneto):
mellow, aromatic white wine served at 50°F / 10°C
Menti bianco (Sicily): dry white wine served at 50°F / 10°C

❖

1 Clean and rinse the fish, place it in a pot, cover with 4 cups water, add salt and pepper, bring to a boil and, frequently skimming it with a slotted spatula, cook for about 20 minutes over moderate heat.

2 Remove from the pot, skin and bone it, and break it up into regular pieces. Filter the cooking broth and set aside. Peel the potatoes, dice them, boil them in a skillet, and drain.

3 Chop the celery and onions and fry in butter in a saucepan, then add the curry and sprinkle in the white flour, stirring constantly with a wooden spoon, and still stirring, add the milk and the filtered broth until you obtain a uniform liquid. Bring the mixture to a boil, add the bay leaves and cook over moderate heat for at least 5 minutes. Finally, add the boiled potatoes and pieces of fish.

4 Adjust the salt and let everything season for another 5 minutes over moderate heat, stirring often. Then serve directly from the pan, sprinkling the minced parsley in at the last minute.

PRACTICAL SUGGESTIONS
This dish can be prepared with salted cod as well. If you do, you should let it soak in water for 24 hours and add less salt.

INGREDIENTS
serves 4

1 1/2 lb. – 700 g COD FILLETS
SALT and PEPPER to taste
2/3 lb. – 250 g POTATOES
1/2 lb. – 200 g CELERY
1/2 lb. – 200 g ONIONS
1/8 cup – 30 g BUTTER
1 teaspoon CURRY
1/3 cup – 40 g WHITE FLOUR
2 cups – 3 dl MILK
2 BAY leaves
1 sprig PARSLEY

EQUIPMENT
a pot
a slotted spatula
a skillet
a saucepan

Difficulty	AVERAGE
Preparation Time	30 MIN.
Cooking Time	45 MIN.
Method of cooking	STOVETOP
Microwave	NO
Freezing	NO
Keeping Time	2 DAYS

SPECIAL NOTE
This dish, imported from Great Britain, is also typical of North American cooking and is generally prepared with shellfish, fish and potatoes.

Pork with Apples

INGREDIENTS

serves 4

1 1/2 lb. – 600 g PORK (neck muscle if
available, known as scamarrita)
4 tablespoons EXTRA VIRGIN OLIVE OIL
1 clove GARLIC
half a teaspoon WILD FENNEL LEAVES
2 cups BROTH
8 WILD APPLES
SALT to taste

EQUIPMENT

a saucepan
a serving dish

Difficulty	AVERAGE
Preparation Time	15 MIN.
Cooking Time	1 HOUR 20 MIN.
Method of cooking	STOVETOP
Microwave	YES
Freezing	YES
Keeping Time	3 DAYS

SPECIAL NOTE

This recipe, typical of the Casentino area of Italy,
uses wild apples, known as *melucce*, as a
fundamental ingredient. These apples are tiny but
extremely flavorful.

RECOMMENDED WINES

Chianti Classico (Tuscany): medium–bodied red wine served at 64°F / 18°C
Alto Adige Grauvernatsch (Alto Adige): light red wine served at 61°F / 16°C

1 Chop the meat into small pieces as if you were making stew. Peel the garlic and cut into four pieces. Place a very small amount of oil in a terra-cotta saucepan, and add the garlic, wild fennel leaves, and the pieces of pork, and sauté.

2 When the meat has browned on all sides, moisten with the broth little by little, and then let it cook about an hour over very low heat, mixing from time to time with a wooden spoon.

3 About 30 minutes before removing the meat from the heat, wash the apples without peeling them, cut them into quarters, remove the core and add to the pork, adjusting the salt.

4 As soon as it's ready, transfer the meat to a serving dish, garnish with apples and serve hot.

PRACTICAL SUGGESTIONS

If you can't find wild apples, this dish will be just as good if you use four rennet apples, which you should cut into rather thick slices as shown in the photo, instead of into quarters.

Cacciucco alla Livornese

INGREDIENTS

serves 6–8

2.2 lb. – I kg ASSORTED SOUP FISH
(angler, hake, mullet, monkfish etc.),
I lb. – 500 g OCTOPUS and SQUID
8 SHRIMP, I lb. – 500 g MUSSELS, thoroughly
cleaned and washed
I ONION, I stalk CELERY, I CARROT
3 cloves GARLIC
2 oz. – I bunch PARSLEY
I pinch HOT RED PEPPER
3 tablespoons EXTRA VIRGIN OLIVE OIL
I cup DRY WHITE WINE
I lb. – 500 g CANNED PLUM TOMATOES
SALT to taste
8 slices STALE HOMEMADE BREAD

EQUIPMENT

a saucepan, a pot
a soup tureen

Difficulty	**ELABORATE**
Preparation Time	**40 MIN.**
Cooking Time	**I HOUR**
Method of cooking	**STOVETOP**
Microwave	**NO**
Freezing	**NO**
Keeping Time	**2 DAYS**

SPECIAL NOTE

Cacciucco is a fish soup made of various fish
cooked over the stove. It usually uses hot red
pepper, known in Livorno as ginger, but which
should not be confused with true ginger.

RECOMMENDED WINES
Bianco Pisano di San Torpé (Tuscany):
mellow, aromatic white wine served at 50°F / 10°C
Colline di Levanto bianco (Liguria):
mellow, aromatic white wine served at 50°F / 10°C

I Clean all the fish, and set aside the heads of the larger ones. Take the prawns out of their shells and clean the octopus and squid. Put the mussels in a saucepan and open the shells; keep only half the shell with the mollusk and the liquid that forms. Mince the onion, the celery, the carrot, the garlic, the parsley and the red pepper and sauté everything in a pot with hot oil. When the mixture begins to brown, add the chopped squid and octopus. Allow the water that forms to evaporate, then moisten with the wine. When it has evaporated, add the crushed tomatoes and a pinch of salt. Continue cooking for another 5 minutes, then remove the squid and octopus and keep them hot (they will become rubbery if they cool).

2 Add the fish heads you set aside to the sauce, along with a cup of hot water, and let them cook for 20 minutes. You should obtain a dense broth that you should strain, squeezing the residue well to get as much substance as possible. Place the puree on the heat again, dilute it with a bit of hot water and add all the remaining raw fish and the prawns. Let it cook over very low heat for at least 15 minutes, then add the octopus, squid and the mussels. Toast the slices of bread in the oven, rub with garlic (if your guests like it) and place them in the soup tureen, pour the cacciucco over them and serve immediately.

PRACTICAL SUGGESTIONS

Instead of serving the cacciucco in one serving dish, you can serve it in individual terra-cotta bowls (which will keep the food hot for a long time), and give each guest 2 slices of toasted bread.

Cima alla Genovese

INGREDIENTS

serves 4–6

2 oz. – 50 g SWEETBREADS
2 oz. – 50 g BRAINS
1 CARROT
1 slice BREAD, with the crust removed
1/2 cup MILK, 1/4 lb. – 100 g SHELLED PEAS
4 EGGS, 3 tablespoons GRATED PARMESAN
2 ONIONS, 1/4 cup – 40 g BUTTER
1/4 lb. – 100 g GROUND LEAN VEAL
2 oz. – 50 g BEEF LOIN (SADDLE)
2 tablespoons PINE NUTS
2 oz. – 1 bunch MINCED MARJORAM
SALT and PEPPER to taste
2 lb. – 800 g VEAL BELLY, cut open
like a pocket

EQUIPMENT

3 bowls, a skillet, 2 saucepans
white kitchen thread and twine, a pot

Difficulty	ELABORATE
Preparation Time	20 MIN.
Cooking Time	1 HOUR 40 MIN.
Method of cooking	STOVETOP
Microwave	NO
Freezing	YES
Keeping Time	3 DAYS

SPECIAL NOTE

In his book *Vera cuciniera genovese* (Real Genovese Cooking), Emanuele Rossi calls this dish "stuffed belly," as it is referred to in certain areas of Piedmont and Lombardy (in Ligurian dialect, *cimma* means belly or bacon).

1 In a saucepan of boiling water, scald the sweetbreads, brains and loin for 5 minutes. Drain, remove the fat and cartilage and cut into pieces. Trim the carrot, peel it, wash it and dice. Soften the bread with milk in a bowl. Cook the peas 3–4 minutes in a skillet of boiling water. In the meantime, beat the eggs with the grated cheese in a bowl. Sauté the onions (washed and finely minced) in a saucepan with the butter, until they have become transparent, but not browned. Add the minced veal to the onions and sauté it over high heat. Add the sweetbreads, brains and saddle, mix and briefly sauté. Add the carrot and peas and season them for a few minutes, mixing with a wooden spoon.

2 Pour the mixture into a mixing bowl, add the drained, squeezed bread, the pine nuts, the marjoram, the eggs beaten with the cheese, salt and pepper, and mix until you have a uniform, very soft mixture. Fill the pocket with the mixture and sew the opening shut. Tie the belly with the kitchen twine. Place the prepared belly in a large saucepan, cover with lightly salted cold water and cook for about an hour and a half. When cooking is complete, remove the belly from the broth and cool between 2 plates under a weight, to retain its original form. Cut the twine when it is cold, slice carefully to avoid crumbling, and serve.

PRACTICAL SUGGESTIONS

The cooking broth will be very good for preparing delicious risotto or soup. If you add a stalk of celery and a carrot while you're cooking the belly, it will be even more flavorful.

Roast Pork in Water

INGREDIENTS

serves 4

3 cloves GARLIC
2 sprigs ROSEMARY
1 2/3 lb. – 800 g PORK LOIN in one piece
SALT and PEPPER to taste

EQUIPMENT

a small bowl
a skillet
kitchen twine
a serving dish

Difficulty	EASY
Preparation Time	10 MIN.
Cooking Time	1 HOUR 30 MIN.
Method of cooking	STOVETOP
Microwave	YES
Freezing	YES
Keeping Time	3 DAYS

SPECIAL NOTE

Boned pork loin is used to prepare roasts and pork chops. In some regions in Italy, the Italian term for pork loin, *lonza*, also refers to a cut of beef, and in other regions it is a sausage similar to loin.

RECOMMENDED WINES
Valcalepio rosso (Lombardy): light red wine served at 64°F / 18°C
Aprilia Merlot (Lazio): light red wine served at 64°F / 18°C

❖

1 Peel the garlic, remove the green shoot in the center, and using a chopping knife, finely mince it with the washed, dried rosemary leaves, then place the minced mixture into a small bowl and set aside.

2 Using a very sharp knife, make deep cuts in the piece of meat and fill them with the minced mixture you prepared. Then tie the loin with kitchen twine and place in a skillet that just barely holds it.

3 Fill with water to barely cover the piece of meat, and cook covered over medium heat for an hour and a half, flavoring with a pinch of salt and freshly ground pepper after it has cooked about 30 minutes.

4 When cooking is complete, the water should be completely absorbed. If it is not, uncover it, raise the heat and let it cook a few more minutes. Remove the roast from the skillet, slice it, place on a serving dish and serve piping hot.

PRACTICAL SUGGESTIONS
You can serve this easy to make dish accompanied by steamed zucchini and carrot rounds, or boiled spinach fried in butter, or mashed potatoes.

Pitaggio

INGREDIENTS

serves 4

1 1/4 lb. – 550 g LIMA BEANS
1 1/4 lb. – 550 g PEAS
3 ARTICHOKES
1 clove GARLIC
1 ONION
6 tablespoons EXTRA VIRGIN OLIVE OIL
SALT and PEPPER to taste
3/4 lb. – 300 g GROUND VEAL
2 tablespoons GRATED PARMESAN
2 oz. – 50 g SOFT BREAD CRUMBS,
soaked in milk
1 EGG
a bit OF WHITE FLOUR

EQUIPMENT

a skillet
a mixing bowl, a frying pan
a serving dish

Difficulty	AVERAGE
Preparation Time	15 MIN.
Cooking Time	50 MIN.
Method of cooking	STOVETOP
Microwave	NO
Freezing	NO
Keeping Time	1 DAY

SPECIAL NOTE

Consumption of lima beans can result in favism, a
serious allergic condition that affects certain
males, even if they come into contact with just
the pollen. The condition was common
in Sardinia and Cilento.

RECOMMENDED WINES
Faro (Sicily): light red wine served at 64°F / 18°C
Sizzano (Piedmont): light red wine served at 64°F / 18°C

1 Shell and wash the lima beans and peas, remove the hard outer
leaves from the artichokes, along with the stalks and any barbs, then
trim and cut into quarters. Peel the garlic and onion, crush the
former and slice the latter.

2 Place the vegetables in a skillet with 2 tablespoons oil, add salt and
pepper and cook about 40 minutes over low heat, covered, then add a
bit of water if necessary.

3 In the meantime, prepare the croquettes. Place the meat in a
mixing bowl, season it with the salt and freshly ground pepper, add
the grated parmesan, the well–squeezed, minced bread , and the egg.

4 Blend well with a wooden spoon and make many small
walnut–sized croquettes with the mixture. Roll in flour and sauté for
10 minutes in a frying pan with the remaining oil, which should be
hot but not boiling.

5 Ten minutes before the vegetables are cooked, add the croquettes
to the skillet, mix and adjust the salt. Transfer to a serving dish and
serve hot.

PRACTICAL SUGGESTIONS
*If you want to make this dish lighter, bake the croquettes in a hot oven
(375°F – 400°F), lightly brushing with olive oil.*

Florentine Meat Loaf

INGREDIENTS

serves 4

2 sprigs PARSLEY

1 clove GARLIC

1 ONION, 2 slices HOMEMADE BREAD

1 cup MILK

1 lb. – 500 g GROUND BEEF

2 EGGS, 2 FRESH SAUSAGES

2 tablespoons – 40 g GRATED PARMESAN

3 tablespoons WHITE FLOUR

1 CARROT

1 stalk CELERY

SALT and PEPPER to taste

5 tablespoons DRY WHITE WINE

1 cup BROTH

juice of one LEMON

EQUIPMENT

a bowl, a mixing bowl

a skillet, a serving dish

Difficulty	**AVERAGE**
Preparation Time	**15 MIN. + 1 HOUR**
Cooking Time	**1 HOUR**
Method of cooking	**STOVETOP**
Microwave	**NO**
Freezing	**YES**
Keeping Time	**3 DAYS**

SPECIAL NOTE

Garlic dilates the small blood vessels, and thus regulates blood pressure and in general improves the circulation. It's also good for anyone suffering from kidney stones.

RECOMMENDED WINES
Chianti (Tuscany): light red wine served at 64°F / 18°C
Dolcetto delle Langhe Monregalesi (Piedmont):
light red wine served at 61°F / 18°C

1 Trim and wash the sprig of parsley, peel the garlic and onion, and using a chopping knife, mince everything together, setting half the onion aside. Soak the slices of bread in a bowl with the milk. Place the meat in a mixing bowl, add the eggs, the soft bread crumbs, squeezed, the minced mixture and the skinned, crumbled sausage. Mix the ingredients into a dough, and shape it into a cylindrical form. Flour it and refrigerate for an hour.

2 Trim and wash the carrot, the stalk of celery and the remaining sprig of parsley, and mince with the remaining half an onion. Sauté the mixture in a skillet, adjust the salt and pepper, then place the meat loaf on it and sauté, turning on all sides. When it is nicely browned, add the white wine and remaining flour, which you have dissolved in a bit of tepid broth (the flour will make the sauce thicker). Cover and lower the heat, then cook slowly for 45 minutes.

3 When cooking is complete, slice the meat loaf and place it on a serving dish, drizzle with lemon juice, then cover with the sauce and serve either hot or cold.

PRACTICAL SUGGESTIONS
This meat loaf can also be wrapped in gauze, tied with thin thread and boiled in lightly salted water. Serve sliced and accompanied by a green sauce (parsley sauce) in its own gravy boat.

Mixed Grilled Meats

RECOMMENDED WINES
Montefalco Sagrantino (Umbria):
medium–bodied red wine served at 64°F / 18°C
Taurasi (Campania): medium–bodied red wine served at 66°F / 19°C

1 Cut the tomatoes in half horizontally and moisten with a bit of oil. Clean the kidneys and remove the fatty part, and place them in a mixing bowl with the sliced liver and a bit of oil, lemon juice, a bit of salt and freshly ground pepper, and marinate 15 minutes.

2 Clean the mushrooms, and if the sausages are fatty (in which case two will be sufficient), cut them in half lengthwise. Heat the grill, and when it is quite hot, place all ingredients on it except for the kidneys, which should be fried in a frying pan for 15 minutes with the sliced bacon and a tablespoon oil.

3 Let all ingredients cook over the hot grill for about 10 minutes on each side, then arrange them on a serving dish. Serve the grilled meats piping hot.

INGREDIENTS
serves 4

2 TOMATOES
4 tablespoons OLIVE OIL
4 LAMB KIDNEYS
4 slices VEAL LIVER
juice of one LEMON
SALT and PEPPER to taste
4 MUSHROOM caps
4 SMALL SAUSAGES (or hot dogs)
4 LAMB CHOPS
4 slices SMOKED BACON

EQUIPMENT
a mixing bowl
a grill
a frying pan
a serving dish

Difficulty	AVERAGE
Preparation Time	20 MIN. + 15 MIN.
Cooking Time	20 MIN.
Method of cooking	GRILL AND STOVETOP
Microwave	NO
Freezing	YES
Keeping Time	2 DAYS

PRACTICAL SUGGESTIONS
Grilled meats can be garnished with sprigs of watercress and slices of lemon, and are traditionally accompanied by French fries, mustard and other sauces. The above meats and organs are suggestions: you can experiment with any meats of your choice.

SPECIAL NOTE
Grilling is quite popular for reasons that include dietary concerns. Not only does it not require seasoning oil, but it also preserves the nutritional properties of the ingredients.

Spinach Meat Loaf

INGREDIENTS

serves 6

1 lb. – 500 g SPINACH
SALT to taste
1 sprig PARSLEY
3 EGGS
3 CARROTS
3/4 lb. – 300 g GROUDN VEAL
1/2 lb. – 200 g HAM
3 tablespoons – 60 g GRATED PARMESAN
2.2 lb. – 1 kg VEAL, cut open like a pocket
1 ONION
1 stalk CELERY
1 BOUILLON CUBE
EXTRA VIRGIN OLIVE OIL to taste

EQUIPMENT

2 pots, a small saucepan
a blender, kitchen thread
a baking dish, a serving dish

Difficulty	**AVERAGE**
Preparation Time	**20 MIN.**
Cooking Time	**1 HOUR 20 MIN.**
Method of cooking	**STOVETOP AND OVEN**
Microwave	**YES**
Freezing	**NO**
Keeping Time	**2 DAYS**

SPECIAL NOTE

According to recent research, celery leaves seem to contain a hormone that has effects similar to insulin, thus making them good for diabetics.

RECOMMENDED WINES
Rosso Conero (Marche): medium–bodied red wine served at 64°F / 18°C
Piave Raboso (Veneto): light red wine served at 64°F / 18°C

1 Cook the spinach in a pot with a small amount of salted water, then drain and squeeze well. Trim and wash the parsley. Hard boil the eggs in a small pan and boil the carrots. Place the minced meat, the ham, the spinach, the parsley and the grated parmesan in a blender. Whip until you have a very uniform mixture.

2 Fill the veal pocket with the prepared mixture and add the hard–boiled eggs and the carrots, arranged nicely (so they have a pleasing appearance when cut into slices). Sew up the pocket with kitchen thread, place it in a pot, cover it well with boiling water and add the onion, celery and the bouillon cube, and cook, covered, for about 50 minutes.

3 When done, remove the meat loaf from the pot, transfer to a lightly oiled baking dish and place in a preheated 355°F oven for about 20 minutes. When it's ready, let it cool, then slice, place on a serving dish and serve.

PRACTICAL SUGGESTIONS

You can accompany this meat loaf with a mixed seasonal vegetable salad, or with steamed new potatoes. If you want to make the dish more flavorful, use an equal amount of lean bacon instead of the ham.

Boiled Meat with Vegetables

INGREDIENTS
serves 6–8

1 lb. – 500 g STRING BEANS
2 ONIONS
2 CLOVES
3 CARROTS
3 POTATOES
1 TURNIP
1 small head of CABBAGE
1/4 cup – 50 g BUTTER
1 CHICKEN weighing about 3 1/2 lb. – 1.5 kg
1 lb. – 500 g BONELESS BEEF
1/2 lb. – 200 g SMOKED SLAB BACON, diced
SALT and PEPPERCORNS to taste
a pinch of THYME

EQUIPMENT
a saucepan, a pot
a slotted spatula, a serving dish

Difficulty	**AVERAGE**
Preparation Time	**30 MIN.**
Cooking Time	**2 HOURS 50 MIN.**
Method of cooking	**STOVETOP**
Microwave	**NO**
Freezing	**YES**
Keeping Time	**1 DAY**

SPECIAL NOTE
Thyme grows wild in the Mediterranean area, but many varieties are also cultivated. One variety, lemon thyme, is especially good for flavoring roast fish.

RECOMMENDED WINES
Sizzano (Piedmont): light red wine served at 64°F / 18°C
Chianti (Tuscany): light red wine served at 64°F / 18°C

1 Carefully trim and wash all vegetables under running water. Using sewing thread, tie the string beans into six bunches. Stick each onion with a clove, chop the carrots and potatoes, cut the turnip in half and the cabbage into quarters. Sauté the butter in a large saucepan, add the chicken and the beef, chopped into pieces, and the diced bacon.

2 Place a large pot of lightly salted water sufficient for the meats and prepared vegetables on the heat, bring to a boil, add the meats and the bacon and boil uncovered, skimming from time to time with a slotted spatula.

3 After two and a quarter hours of slow cooking, add all the vegetables to the broth along with a few peppercorns and the thyme, and if necessary adjust the salt and cook for 30 minutes more. Finally, drain the broth and serve the boiled meats in a large serving dish surrounded by the vegetables.

PRACTICAL SUGGESTIONS
The cooking broth for the boiled meats can be served in a cup or used for another occasion. The smoked bacon can be substituted with normal bacon, provided it is rather lean.

Roast with Sage

INGREDIENTS
serves 4

1 1/3 LB. – 600 G PORK (fillet or tenderloin)
1 clove GARLIC
SALT and PEPPER to taste
6 leaves and a sprig SAGE
5 tablespoons EXTRA VIRGIN OLIVE OIL

For the side dish
MASHED POTATOES as necessary

EQUIPMENT
white kitchen thread
an oval baking dish
a serving dish

Difficulty	**AVERAGE**
Preparation Time	**10 MIN.**
Cooking Time	**1 HOUR 20 MIN.**
Method of cooking	**OVEN**
Microwave	**YES**
Freezing	**YES**
Keeping Time	**3 DAYS**

SPECIAL NOTE
To Romans, sage was a sacred plant. The person designated to gather it had to make a sacrifice of bread and wine, then wear a white tunic and have clean, bare feet.

RECOMMENDED WINES
Barbera d'Alba (Piedmont): light red wine served at 64°F / 18°C
Vino Nobile di Montepulciano (Tuscany):
medium–bodied red wine served at 64°F / 18°C

1 Tie the meat with white kitchen thread. Chop the garlic into small pieces and add salt and pepper. Using a very sharp knife, make cuts in the meat, into which you should add pieces of garlic and minced sage leaves.

2 Wash and dry the sprig of sage and place it in a baking dish with the oil and meat. Preheat the oven to 375°F – 400°F, place the baking dish in it and brown the meat uniformly for 20 minutes, then lower the heat and continue baking for about an hour, basting it occasionally.

3 Serve the roast sliced, in a serving dish, surrounded by hot mashed potatoes. Remove the sprig of sage from the cooking juices and serve the juices separately.

PRACTICAL SUGGESTIONS
If the cooking juices are too liquid, fifteen minutes before serving the meat, add a scant tablespoon of flour well blended with a tablespoon butter, or a tablespoon cornstarch dissolved in a little water.

Tapulone

INGREDIENTS

serves 4

1 lb. GROUND BEEF
1 oz. – 20 g MINCED BACON
1/4 cup – 40 g BUTTER
or 3 tablespoons olive oil
1 WHITE ONION
1/2 teaspoon WHITE FLOUR
ASSORTED POWDERED SPICES (a dash)
4 CLOVES
half a BAY leaf
SALT and PEPPER to taste
1 cup RED WINE

EQUIPMENT

a meat grinder
a terra–cotta pan

Difficulty	AVERAGE
Preparation Time	30 MIN.
Cooking Time	1 HOUR 30 MIN.
Method of cooking	STOVETOP
Microwave	NO
Freezing	NO
Keeping Time	3 DAYS

SPECIAL NOTE

Ground beef should always be cooked with
ingredients like red wine and herbs and spices
that cut the fat.

RECOMMENDED WINES
Ghemme (Piedmont): medium–bodied red wine served at 64°F / 18°C
Colli Orientali del Friuli Refosco dal peduncolo rosso (Friuli Venezia
Giulia): light red wine served at 64°F / 18°C

1 Remove the fat and skin from the meat and chop it coarsely with
a knife, or else use a meat grinder, using the cutting blade with the
largest grinding holes. Using a chopping knife, mince the bacon.

2 Melt the butter (or heat the oil) in the skillet, adding the
previously peeled and minced onion, allow it to become golden
without browning, add the bacon, mix with a wooden spoon to
season it, then add the meat, raise the heat and continue stirring
until well browned.

3 Add the flour and stir until everything is absorbed. Add the
spices, the cloves, the bay leaf, a pinch of salt and freshly ground
pepper, and cover with wine.

4 Cover, lower the heat and cook about an hour and a half, stirring
occasionally to prevent the flour from making the preparation stick
to the bottom of the skillet. When done, the meat should be well-
cooked and the sauce reduced.

PRACTICAL SUGGESTIONS
Tapulone is a rather fatty dish, and works very well with polenta prepared
with coarse Bergamo cornmeal. If you prefer a lighter dish, let it cool to
lukewarm, remove the fatty part that floats to the surface, return to the heat
and serve piping hot in the pan.

Mutton Spiedini

INGREDIENTS
serves 4

2 1/2 lb. – 700 g MUTTON LEG, diced
1/2 lb. – 200 g ONIONS, cut into rounds
1 level teaspoon POWDERED THYME
a few BAY leaves
6 tablespoons EXTRA VIRGIN OLIVE OIL
HOMEMADE BREAD as necessary,
cut into small squares
1 EGGPLANT, cubed
SALT and PEPPER to taste

For the side dish
3/4 lb. – 300 g rice, either vialone or carnaroli

EQUIPMENT
a mixing bowl
8 metal skewers or sturdy wood sticks
a grill, a pot, a serving dish

Difficulty	AVERAGE
Preparation Time	20 MIN. + 6 HOURS
Cooking Time	30 MIN.
Method of cooking	GRILL
Microwave	YES
Freezing	NO
Keeping Time	2 DAYS

SPECIAL NOTE
The word kebab is used in the Middle East to Northern India. Kebabs are roasted over a bright flame, on wood coals, or even in the oven or grilled.

Recommended Wines
Biferno rosso (Molise): light red wine served at 64°F / 18°C
Carmignano (Tuscany): medium–bodied red wine served at 64°F / 18°C

1 Wash and dry the cubed meat, place it in a mixing bowl, add the onions, sliced into rounds, the powdered thyme, and the bay leaves cut in two. Moisten with oil, mix, cover and let the meat marinate at least 6 hours.

2 Take out the cubed meat, skewer it on the sticks, alternating with the halved bay leaves, the squares of homemade bread and the cubes of eggplant.

3 Heat the grill well, place the spiedini on it and cook, turning on each side and occasionally moistening with a bit of the marinade.

4 Cook the rice in a pot with a generous amount of salted boiling water, then place it on a serving dish piping hot, place the mutton spiedini on top, with salt and pepper added when done, drizzle everything with the remaining marinade, then serve hot immediately.

Practical Suggestions
These spiedini are like those offered in Middle Eastern restaurants, where they are called kebabs. *If you want more flavorful shish kebabs that do not follow Muslim tradition, which forbids pork, you can add cubed fatty and lean prosciutto and a few sliced tomatoes.*

Freshwater Fish Tegamaccio

INGREDIENTS

serves 4

1 sprig PARSLEY
1 stalk CELERY
1 ONION
4 cloves GARLIC
4 tablespoons EXTRA VIRGIN OLIVE OIL
1 lb. – 400 g EEL, cleaned and chopped
1/2 lb. – 200 g PIKE, sliced
1/2 lb. – 200 g TOMATO SAUCE
SALT to taste
1/2 lb. – 200 g PERCH FILLETS
4 slices HOMEMADE BREAD

EQUIPMENT

a saucepan
a serving dish

Difficulty	**AVERAGE**
Preparation Time	**15 MIN.**
Cooking Time	**1 HOUR**
Method of cooking	**STOVETOP**
Microwave	**NO**
Freezing	**NO**
Keeping Time	**1 DAY**

SPECIAL NOTE

Freshwater perch lives in the lakes of northern Italy and much of Europe. Its flesh is excellent, but its eggs are toxic.

RECOMMENDED WINES
Alto Adige Pinot bianco (Trentino Alto Adige):
dry white wine served at 50°F / 10°C
Colli Perugini bianco (Umbria): dry white wine served at 50°F / 10°C

1 Trim and wash the parsley and the stalk of celery; peel the onion and a clove of garlic. Mince these vegetables and place in a saucepan, preferably of terra–cotta, with the oil. Fry, and when the onion grows golden brown, add the eel.

2 After cooking for about 10 minutes, add the slices of pike and the tomato sauce. Add salt, cover and cook over low heat for another 20 minutes. During cooking, avoid stirring, but shake the pan from time to time. After 20 minutes, add the perch fillets.

3 In the meantime, cut the slices of bread in two and toast in the oven. Peel the remaining cloves of garlic, cut in half vertically, remove the green shoot in the center, and rub on the hot slices of bread. Place the slices on a serving dish.

4 Cook the mixture 10 more minutes after adding the perch, then remove from the heat and pour the fish with the sauce onto the slices of bread. Serve immediately piping hot.

PRACTICAL SUGGESTIONS
The fish needs to be very fresh for this dish to be successful. You can also serve it in individual bowls, placing a slice of bread in each one and then pouring in a bit of fish and sauce.

Dried Cod in Potacchio

Bianchello del Metauro (Marche): dry white wine served at 50°F / 10°C
Castel del Monte rosato (Puglia): rosé served at 50°F / 10°C

1 Pound the dried cod with the meat pounder and soak it in a large bowl of cold water for 2 days, being sure to change the water often. After draining it, dry it well with a kitchen cloth, remove the bones and chop into pieces.

2 Peel the onion and slice it thinly. Place it in a casserole and sauté in the oil over low heat, without letting it brown. Drain the anchovies from the oil. Trim the parsley and wash it. Remove the rosemary leaves from the sprig. Peel the clove of garlic and mince it with all the herbs.

3 When the onion is sautéed well, add the minced herbs, mixing with a wooden spoon and seasoning a few minutes. Scald the tomatoes in boiling water, skin them, cut in half, remove the seeds and cut the pulp into pieces.

4 Add the tomatoes to the skillet, mix and cook 5–6 minutes. Then add the pieces of dried cod and cook (about 2 hours) over low heat. When cooking is half done, moisten with the wine, and add salt and pepper to taste. If necessary during cooking, add a bit of hot water.

PRACTICAL SUGGESTIONS
Cook the dried cod as long as it takes to become tender. Many believe (rightly) that it is also excellent reheated the next day.

INGREDIENTS
serves 4

1 lb. – 400 g DRIED COD
or 2 lb. – 800 g softened dried cod
1 ONION
3 tablespoons EXTRA VIRGIN OLIVE OIL
4 ANCHOVY FILLETS IN OIL
1 sprig PARSLEY
1 sprig ROSEMARY
1 clove GARLIC
3/4 lb. – 300 g ripe TOMATOES
1 cup DRY WHITE WINE
SALT and PEPPER to taste

EQUIPMENT
a meat pounder
a mixing bowl
a skillet

Difficulty	AVERAGE
Preparation Time	20 MIN. + 2 DAYS
Cooking Time	2 HOURS
Method of cooking	STOVETOP
Microwave	YES
Freezing	YES
Keeping Time	3 DAYS

SPECIAL NOTE
Typical of the cuisine of the Marche region of Italy, *potacchio*, from the French *potage*, is not a soup but a thick, saucy dish. It can be prepared with chicken and lamb as well as with dried cod.

Hake with Herbs

INGREDIENTS

serves 4

4 HAKE FILLETS (total of 1 1/3 lb. – 600 g)
3/4 lb. – 300 g POTATOES
1 ONION
1 sprig PARSLEY
1 clove GARLIC
1 sprig ROSEMARY
2 leaves SAGE
1 sprig THYME
4 tablespoons EXTRA VIRGIN OLIVE OIL
5 tablespoons DRY WHITE WINE
SALT to taste
SAFFRON as necessary

EQUIPMENT

a saucepan
absorbent paper towels

Difficulty	AVERAGE
Preparation Time	15 MIN.
Cooking Time	15 MIN.
Method of cooking	STOVETOP
Microwave	YES
Freezing	NO
Keeping Time	1 DAY

SPECIAL NOTE

Saffron is very costly, as 80 pounds of flowers
produce only one pound of fresh saffron and just
under 3 ounces of powdered saffron.

RECOMMENDED WINES
Capri bianco (Campania): dry white wine served at 50°F / 10°C
Santa Margherita di Belice bianco (Sicily):
dry white wine served at 50°F / 10°C

1 Wash the hake fillets and dry them gently with a cloth or absorbent paper towels. Peel the potatoes, wash them in abundant cold water, drain, dry with a dishtowel and cut into pieces.

2 Peel the onion and wash and slice finely. Wash the parsley leaves. Peel the garlic and finely mince the parsley with the garlic, rosemary, sage and thyme.

3 Pour the oil into a large pot. Add the sliced onion and pieces of potato and sprinkle with the minced herbs. Moisten the mixture with a water glass of white wine.

4 Slowly bring to a boil and cook 7–8 minutes, or until the potatoes are tender. Add the hake fillets, season with salt and sprinkle with a bit of saffron.

5 Continue cooking over moderate heat, covered, for 6–7 minutes, occasionally basting the fillets with the cooking sauce. Serve hot.

PRACTICAL SUGGESTIONS
This dish is also excellent with other types of fish, even frozen fish. You can use dab, cod, and others.

74

Sole Kebabs

INGREDIENTS

serves 4

2 ZUCCHINI
4 tablespoons EXTRA VIRGIN OLIVE OIL
4 SOLE FILLETS
2 oz. – I bunch PARSLEY, minced
SALT and PEPPER to taste
3/4 lb. – 300 g firm, ripe TOMATOES
I YELLOW BELL PEPPER
I teaspoon PAPRIKA

For the side dish
RICE PILAF as necessary

EQUIPMENT

a grill
a saucepan
a skillet
4 wooden skewers

Difficulty	AVERAGE
Preparation Time	35 MIN.
Cooking Time	20 MIN.
Method of cooking	GRILL
Microwave	NO
Freezing	NO
Keeping Time	I DAY

SPECIAL NOTE

Pilaf is a typical method for preparing rice in the Balkans and Middle East. The best types of rice for making pilaf are hard grain varieties.

RECOMMENDED WINES
Friuli Grave Pinot bianco (Friuli Venezia Giulia):
dry white wine served at 50°F / 10°C
Viganello Greco (Lazio): mellow, aromatic white wine served at 50°F / 10°C

I Trim and wash the zucchini, cut them into rounds and lightly brush with oil. Place on a preheated grill and grill for a minute, turning once, then remove and set aside. Keep the grill very hot. Wash the sole fillets, dry them gently and cut each one into three pieces. Place them on a flat surface, sprinkle with minced parsley, salt and a grind of pepper, and roll up.

2 Prepare the shish kebabs: skewer 3 fillets on each skewer, alternating with the zucchini rounds, brush with a little oil, sprinkle with a pinch of salt and a grind of pepper, place on the hot grill and cook 3–4 minutes, turning on all sides.

3 Scald the tomatoes in a saucepan of boiling water. Drain, peel, remove the seeds and vegetable water, then cut into cubes. Wash the pepper, cut in half, remove the seeds and white part and cut into cubes. Place the tomato cubes and the pepper in a skillet with the remaining oil, add the paprika, the salt and the pepper and cook 5 minutes over high heat, stirring occasionally. Serve the shish kebabs hot, accompanied by the tomato and pepper cubes and as much rice pilaf as you like.

PRACTICAL SUGGESTIONS

Cook rice pilaf as follows: melt the butter in a saucepan that can be put in the oven, add the onion and wilt it. Add the rice, add salt, pour in hot broth, mix for a minute, then cover and place in the oven for 20 minutes without removing the cover.

Bass with Fennel

INGREDIENTS

serves 4

1 BASS
weighing about 2.5 lb. – 1.2 kilos
2 FENNEL BULBS
2 tablespoons LEMON JUICE
2 tablespoons EXTRA VIRGIN OLIVE OIL
SALT and PEPPER to taste

EQUIPMENT

a mixing bowl
a baking pan
aluminum foil
a serving dish

Difficulty	AVERAGE
Preparation Time	15 MIN.
Cooking Time	30 MIN.
Method of cooking	OVEN
Microwave	NO
Freezing	NO
Keeping Time	1 DAY

SPECIAL NOTE

Bass is a sea fish with firm, white, very good quality meat. Common in the Mediterranean and eastern Atlantic, it can also be found in salt lakes and the mouths of rivers.

RECOMMENDED WINES
Collio goriziano Müller Thurgau (Friuli–Venezia Giulia):
dry white wine served at 50°F / 10°C
Orvieto (Umbria): mellow, aromatic white wine served at 50°F / 10°C

1 Prepare the bass for cooking. Wash it under running water and dry it. Trim the fennel, eliminating the outer portion and tips, then cut in half. Wash under running water and slice as thinly as possible.

2 Place the sliced fennel in a mixing bowl and season with the lemon juice, oil, a pinch of salt and a bit of freshly ground white pepper, then turn a number of times to season it well.

3 Place a few fennel slices and the seasoning on a sheet of aluminum foil. Place the bass on top and cover it with the remaining fennel.

4 Seal the ends of the foil, place it in a baking pan and bake in a preheated 400°F oven for about 30 minutes. When cooking is complete, remove the bass from the oven, remove the aluminum foil, transfer the fish to a serving dish, surround it with the fennel and serve piping hot.

PRACTICAL SUGGESTIONS
When you clean the bass, be very careful when gutting it, because this fish likes to eat small crustaceans, the remains of which could easily cut your finger and even cause an infection.

Stewed Sturgeon

INGREDIENTS

serves 4

2.2 lb. – I kg STURGEON, sliced
I sprig PARSLEY
SALT and PEPPER to taste
I cup EXTRA VIRGIN OLIVE OIL
2 cups DRY WHITE WINE
4 ANCHOVIES IN SALT
2 ONIONS or LEEKS
2 cloves GARLIC
I stalk CELERY
I teaspoon DRY MARJORAM
2 BAY leaves
3/4 lb. – 300 g PLUM TOMATOES

EQUIPMENT

a mixing bowl
a saucepan
a serving dish

Difficulty	**AVERAGE**
Preparation Time	**20 MIN. + 2 HOURS**
Cooking Time	**35 MIN.**
Method of cooking	**STOVETOP**
Microwave	**YES**
Freezing	**NO**
Keeping Time	**I DAY**

SPECIAL NOTE

Sturgeon is available in Italy through fish farms, but the Russian rivers that flow into the Caspian Sea and the Black Sea still hold a monopoly.

RECOMMENDED WINES
Collio goriziano Sauvignon (Friuli–Venezia Giulia):
mellow, aromatic white wine served at 50°F / 10°C
Vernaccia di Oristano (Sardinia):
mellow, aromatic white wine served at 50°F / 10°C

I Wash the sturgeon well and place in a mixing bowl. Sprinkle with the washed, minced parsley, a pinch of salt and a bit of freshly ground pepper. Moisten with half the oil and the wine and marinate about 2 hours, turning it a number of times to season well.

2 In the meantime, remove the salt from the anchovies, bone them and chop into pieces. Peel the onions and garlic. Scrape and wash the celery stalk, and using a chopping knife, mince everything together. Sauté the minced mixture in a saucepan with the other half of the oil, the marjoram, the bay leaf and the anchovies.

3 Season for a few minutes, then add the slices of sturgeon drained well from the marinade (which you should set aside). Brown them well and add the tomatoes. When the sauce becomes quite thick, dilute it with the remaining wine and marinade, and cook about 20 minutes.

4 Transfer the sliced fish to a serving dish, season with the cooking sauce and serve hot, accompanied by white or yellow polenta if you like.

PRACTICAL SUGGESTIONS

If the cooking liquid is too thin, remove the fish, run the mixture through a fine sieve, put it back in the baking dish and reduce over moderate heat, until it becomes thick enough.

Trout Salad

INGREDIENTS

serves 4

1 ONION, 3 CARROTS, 1 stalk CELERY
1 sprig PARSLEY, 1 sprig THYME
1 BAY leaf, SALT and PEPPERCORNS to taste
3–4 tablespoons DRY WHITE WINE
1 TROUT, weighing about 2.5 lb. – 1.2 kg, cleaned
2 POTATOES, 1/2 lb. – 200 g GREEN ONIONS
1/2 lb. – 200 g BRUSSELS SPROUTS
1/2 lb. – 200 g SQUASH

For the seasoning
3 ANCHOVIES IN SALT
1/2 tablespoon CAPERS IN SALT
4 tablespoons EXTRA VIRGIN OLIVE OIL
2 tablespoons WHITE WINE VINEGAR
SALT to taste

EQUIPMENT

2 pots, a baking sheet
a mixing bowl, a bowl

Difficulty	**AVERAGE**
Preparation Time	**20 MIN.**
Cooking Time	**1 HOUR 20 MIN.**
Method of cooking	**STOVETOP AND OVEN**
Microwave	**NO**
Freezing	**NO**
Keeping Time	**1 DAY**

SPECIAL NOTE

Commercial farm trout has a softer flesh than brook trout, but this can be avoided by raising them in tanks traversed by strong currents of water that can sometimes be carried in from a nearby river.

RECOMMENDED WINES
Erbaluce di Caluso (Piedmont): dry white wine served at 50°F / 10°C
Bianchello del Metauro (Marche): dry white wine served at 50°F / 10°C

1 Peel the onion, wash the carrots, the stalk of celery and the aromatic herbs. Place them in a pot with 1 quart – 2 liters salted water with the peppercorns, and bring to a boil. When the water comes to a boil, add the wine, wait for it to begin boiling again, and place the trout in the pot. Cook covered for 25–30 minutes, then turn off the heat and let the fish cool in its cooking broth. In the meantime, peel the potatoes and chop into small chunks. Peel the green onions. Trim the Brussels sprouts and wash. Cook these vegetables for about 20 minutes in a pot of salted boiling water. Cut the squash into small chunks, place on a baking sheet without adding any seasoning, and cook 15–20 minutes.

2 Remove the trout, which by now has cooled, from its cooking broth, and place the meat only in a mixing bowl (being careful not to leave in any bones), and cut into large pieces. Add the well drained vegetables, and mix well. Remove the salt and bones from the anchovies, break them into pieces and work with a wooden spoon in a bowl. Remove the salt from the capers, mince finely and add to the anchovies. Add the oil, mix, emulsify with the vinegar and season the trout salad with this dressing.

PRACTICAL SUGGESTIONS
Clean the trout as follows: scale it with a knife by scraping the skin without breaking it, working from the tail to the head. Gut it by making an incision in the belly with a scissors and grasp the entrails, which will come out in one mass. Remove the fins and wash the trout in running water, then cook as indicated in the recipe.

Galician Pescado

INGREDIENTS

serves 6

1 GREEN PEPPER

1/4 lb. — 100 g MUSHROOMS

2 finely minced ONIONS

1 GREEN ONION

2 ripe TOMATOES

12 FILLETS OF FISH

SALT and PEPPER to taste

pinch of PAPRIKA

pinch of NUTMEG

3 tablespoons OLIVE OIL

1 clove GARLIC

12 ANCHOVY fillets

2 cups DRY WHITE WINE

1 oz. — 20 g BUTTER

EQUIPMENT

a small saucepan, a baking dish

Difficulty	AVERAGE
Preparation Time	40 MIN.
Cooking Time	35 MIN.
Method of cooking	STOVETOP AND OVEN
Microwave	YES
Freezing	YES
Keeping Time	1 DAY

SPECIAL NOTE

Paprika is a spice that became popular in Balkan cooking during Turkish domination. It is widely used in Hungarian cooking, for example in the very popular dish, goulash.

RECOMMENDED WINES
Bianco di Custoza (Veneto): dry white wine served at 50°F / 10°C
Isonzo Malvasia istriana (Friuli–Venezia Giulia):
mellow, aromatic white wine served at 50°F / 10°C

1 Wash the pepper, remove the seeds and white portion, and cut into strips. Remove the earthy part of the mushrooms, wash rapidly and slice thinly. Finely mince the two onions and green onion. Scald the tomatoes for a minute in boiling water, then skin, remove the seeds and vegetable water and slice.

2 Wash and dry the fish fillets. Season with salt, freshly ground pepper, paprika and nutmeg. Heat the oil in a baking dish, add the minced onion, the clove of garlic and the strips of pepper, and heat until wilted.

3 Sauté everything for 5 minutes, occasionally mixing with a wooden spoon, then add the fish fillets. Brown them on both sides and place an anchovy fillet, a slice of tomato, a bit of minced green onion and some slices of mushrooms on each one. Drizzle with the white wine.

4 Preheat the oven to 450°F and bake the fish 20–25 minutes, adding the melted butter at the last minute. Serve piping hot directly from the baking dish.

PRACTICAL SUGGESTIONS
To prepare this Spanish dish, you can use various types of fish fillets. Some examples are small cod or mullet. If you like, before serving, sprinkle with minced parsley.

Trapani-Style Couscous

RECOMMENDED WINES
Etna bianco (Sicily): dry white wine served at 50°F / 10°C
Nasco di Cagliari secco (Sardinia): dry white wine served at 50°F / 10°C

1 To prepare the flour: moisten with a very small amount water, salt lightly and rub between the palms of your hands. When it has separated into small granules, drop it into the special pot (*mafaradda*) and steam cook for about 45 minutes.

2 Prepare the fish: clean and wash the fish and chop into pieces. Fry the onions in the oil with the garlic and parsley; add the bay leaf and tomatoes.

3 Place the fish into the pot and barely cover with water. Add salt and pepper, dissolve the saffron in a bit of hot water and add it to the preparation with the almonds.

4 Cook the fish over moderate heat. When it is quite done and the sauce has thickened, remove from the heat. Moisten the flour with some of the cooking sauce. Place the fish in the center of a large serving dish and pour the remaining sauce over it. Surround with the couscous and serve.

PRACTICAL SUGGESTIONS
You can find precooked semolina flour that will allow you to prepare couscous rapidly. To balance this single-dish meal, serve with your favorite cooked vegetables.

INGREDIENTS
serves 6

1 lb. – 500 g SEMOLINA FLOUR
SALT and PEPPER to taste
about 1 3/4 lb. – 1.3 kg MIXED FISH (eel, grouper, dentex, scorpionfish, etc.)
2 sliced ONIONS
6 tablespoons EXTRA VIRGIN OLIVE OIL
1 clove GARLIC, minced
1 tablespoon minced PARSLEY
1 BAY leaf
3–4 ripe TOMATOES, chopped
1/4 teaspoon SAFFRON
2 oz. – 50 g GROUND ALMONDS

EQUIPMENT
1 couscous pot, known as a *mafaradda*
a skillet
a serving dish

Difficulty	AVERAGE
Preparation Time	35 MIN.
Cooking Time	1 HOUR 15 MIN.
Method of cooking	STOVETOP
Microwave	NO
Freezing	NO
Keeping Time	2 DAYS

SPECIAL NOTE
Couscous is a North African dish that is very common in Mediterranean Europe. It consists of steam-cooked semolina flour mixed with water.

Fennel Soufflé   p88

Baked Belgian Endive   p89

Eggplant with Caciocavallo   p90

Fried Au Gratin Potatoes   p92

Bagna Caôda   p94

Spinach Strudel   p96

Baked Zucchini   p98

Florentine Pie   p100

Cabbage and Potatoes   p101

Chard Stalks Parmesan   p102

Au Gratin Tomatoes   p104

Mushroom Croquettes   p106

Eggplant Parmesan   p108

Stuffed Bell Peppers   p110

Stuffed Cabbage p112

Stuffed Endive Bundles p113

Leeks with Cheese p114

Potato Pie p116

Cavolata p118

Squash with Beans p120

Mushroom Caps on Grape Leaves p122

Vegetables

Fennel Soufflé

INGREDIENTS

serves 4

For the béchamel

1/4 cup — 50 g BUTTER

1/3 cup — 50 g WHITE FLOUR

2 cups — 5 dl MILK

SALT to taste

1 pinch NUTMEG

3 1/3 lb. — 1.5 kg FENNEL

SALT and PEPPER to taste

2 tablespoons — 20 g GRATED PARMESAN

2 EGGS

1/8 cup — 20 g BUTTER

EQUIPMENT

a pot, a skillet

a double boiler

a mixing bowl, a baking dish

Difficulty	**ELABORATE**
Preparation Time	**20 MIN.**
Cooking Time	**1 HOUR 10 MIN.**
Method of cooking	**STOVETOP AND OVEN**
Microwave	**NO**
Freezing	**NO**
Keeping Time	**1 DAY**

SPECIAL NOTE

Fennel is a vegetable that has had its ups and downs. It was appreciated by the Greeks and Romans solely for its medicinal qualities, and did not make its first appearance on a Florentine table until the 15th century.

1 Prepare the béchamel by melting the butter in a skillet without browning it, then adding the flour (sprinkling it in very slowly) and stirring constantly with a wooden spoon to prevent lumps from forming. Cook the mixture for about 5 minutes over high heat, then add the milk slowly, stirring until it has completely blended. Continue cooking for 10 minutes, adjusting the salt and sprinkling with a pinch of freshly grated nutmeg.

2 Clean the fennel and boil them 15 minutes in a generous amount of salted water, then drain and, using a chopping knife, mince them finely. Transfer to a mixing bowl, add the béchamel, the parmesan, 2 egg yolks (setting the whites aside), a pinch of salt and freshly ground pepper and mix well to blend everything.

3 Beat the egg whites to stiff peaks and add to the mixture in the bowl, folding them in gently until you have a creamy, uniform mixture. Generously butter a baking dish and pour in the prepared mixture. Place the pan in a double boiler and bake about 40 minutes without opening the oven, checking from the outside to see that it has become golden brown. Serve immediately in the baking dish to prevent the soufflé from collapsing..

PRACTICAL SUGGESTIONS

For this dish to be successful, the fennel must be young and tender. If you're in a hurry, you can boil them the day before and keep them in the refrigerator, wrapped in plastic.

Baked Belgian Endive with Sliced Cheese

RECOMMENDED WINES
*Colli Piacentini Val di Nure (Emilia–Romagna):
dry white wine served at 50°F / 10°C
Colli del Trasimeno bianco (Umbria): dry white wine served at 50°F / 10°C*

1 Preheat the oven to 400°F. Heat a generous amount of water in a skillet, if possible oval in shape, and salt it as it comes to a boil. Remove the wilted or broken leaves of the endive, then, using a corer, remove the core, which is very bitter. Wash the heads and toss into the boiling water.

2 Cook the endive about 5 minutes, uncovered, carefully drain it, and then place it on a kitchen towel and press lightly to remove as much water as possible. Then allow it to cool.

3 In the meantime, brown the minced onion in a small saucepan with the butter, over low heat, and pour half of this mixture into a rectangular baking dish large enough to hold the endive in a single layer. Wrap the central portion of each head with a slice of cheese, and arrange them in the baking dish. Wilt the remaining onion in the butter and distribute on each of them.

4 Pour on a few tablespoons cream and sprinkle everything with grated parmesan. Place a piece of aluminum foil over the baking dish (without sealing the sides), and bake about 10 minutes. Remove, and as soon as the surface is lightly browned, remove, transfer to a serving dish and serve.

PRACTICAL SUGGESTIONS
When you buy Belgian endive, select heads that are about the same size, so cooking will be uniform. To eliminate its bitter taste, add a piece of dry bread to the cooking water.

INGREDIENTS
serves 4

SALT to taste
8 heads BELGIAN ENDIVE
1 medium ONION
1/8 cup — 30 g BUTTER
8 slices PROCESSED CHEESE
a few tablespoons LIQUID CREAM
GRATED PARMESAN as necessary

EQUIPMENT
a skillet
a corer
a pot
a small saucepan
aluminum foil
a rectangular baking dish
a serving dish

Difficulty	AVERAGE
Preparation Time	15 MIN.
Cooking Time	18 MIN. – 20 MIN.
Method of cooking	STOVETOP AND OVEN
Microwave	YES
Freezing	NO
Keeping Time	1 DAY

SPECIAL NOTE
Belgian endive was first cultivated in 1850, when a certain Bréziers, a Brussels gardener, had the idea of cultivating chicory in the caves where mushrooms were grown.

Eggplant with Caciocavallo

INGREDIENTS
serves 4

4 EGGPLANTS
SALT and PEPPER to taste
1 pinch POWDERED CARAWAY
3/4 lb. – 300 g SHARP CACIOCAVALLO
(a gourd-shaped cheese from Southern Italy),
sliced
SUNFLOWER SEED OIL for frying

For the batter
1/2 lb. – 200 g WHITE FLOUR
2 EGGS
1 tablespoon OLIVE OIL

EQUIPMENT
a mixing bowl, a frying pan
absorbent paper towels
a serving dish

Difficulty	AVERAGE
Preparation Time	20 MIN. + 2 HOURS
Cooking Time	15 MIN.
Method of cooking	STOVETOP
Microwave	YES
Freezing	YES
Keeping Time	2 DAYS

SPECIAL NOTE
Caraway has been found in remains of food
dating back to the Stone Age. The name comes
from the Arabic *karawija*, which referred
to the seed.

RECOMMENDED WINES
Montepulciano d'Abruzzo (Abruzzi): light red wine served at 64°F / 18°C
San Severo rosato (Puglia): rosé served at 54°F / 12°C

1 Peel the eggplant and chop into rather thin slices. Sprinkle with salt, place into a colander and allow it to expel the vegetation water. After an hour, wash it under running water and dry. Sprinkle a pinch of pepper and one of caraway on each slice of cheese, and place each one between two slices of eggplant. Form a sort of sandwich, pressing firmly on the edges to keep them together.

2 Prepare the batter by mixing the flour with two cups of tepid water in a mixing bowl. Beat the eggs with a fork and add them to the mixture, along with the olive oil. Let it sit for at least an hour.

3 Dip the eggplant and cheese "sandwiches" in the batter, allow any extra to drip off, and fry them in a pan of hot oil. Brown on both sides, then place on a paper towel to eliminate any excess oil, transfer to a serving dish and serve immediately, piping hot.

PRACTICAL SUGGESTIONS
Use little fat when cooking eggplant: enough to prevent the slices from sticking to the bottom of the pan, but a little less than would seem necessary when you start frying. A nonstick frying pan that you can barely brush with oil would work very well.

90

Fried Au Gratin Potatoes

INGREDIENTS

serves 4

1 lb. — 500 g POTATOES
4 tablespoons EXTRA VIRGIN OLIVE OIL
SALT to taste
1 sprig PARSLEY

EQUIPMENT

a saucepan
a serving dish

Difficulty	**AVERAGE**
Preparation Time	**20 MIN.**
Cooking Time	**30 MIN.**
Method of cooking	**STOVETOP**
Microwave	**YES**
Freezing	**NO**
Keeping Time	**1 DAY**

SPECIAL NOTE

A raw potato placed among heather, for example, will keep the plant green for a long time. Potato cooking water can be used to clean silver; soak it in the water for 2 hours.

RECOMMENDED WINES
Colli di Parma (Emilia–Romagna): light red wine served at 61°F / 16°C
Colline Novaresi Vespolina (Piedmont): light red wine served at 61°F / 16°C

1 Peel the potatoes, wash well, dry and slice into thin rounds that are as uniform as possible. Heat the oil in a large saucepan. Add the potatoes and spread them out uniformly.

2 Salt everything uniformly, as the potatoes will not be mixed. Raise the heat for a few minutes to brown the bottom of the potatoes.

3 Turn the heat back to moderate and cook about 25 minutes, without turning or touching the potatoes. Then turn the potatoes over onto a serving dish and decorate with a few leaves of washed, dried parsley.

PRACTICAL SUGGESTIONS
To make the dish softer, brush the potato rounds with extra virgin olive oil before placing them in the pan. If you want to make it a little richer, add a few cubed pieces of sliced bacon or prosciutto that you have sautéed in the frying pan for a few minutes.

Bagna Caôda

INGREDIENTS

serves 6

1/3 cup — 70 g BUTTER
12 cloves GARLIC
3/4 lb. — 300 g ANCHOVY FILLETS,
boned and with the salt removed
3/4 cup — 3 dl EXTRA VIRGIN OLIVE OIL
1 bunch CARDOONS (optional)
2 RAW OR ROASTED BELL PEPPERS
3 JERUSALEM ARTICHOKES (sunchokes)
1 bunch CELERY
1 FENNEL
1 CAULIFLOWER
2 ARTICHOKES, cut into wedges
a few leaves WHITE CABBAGE

EQUIPMENT

a terra-cotta saucepan
a chaffing dish
a serving dish

Difficulty	**AVERAGE**
Preparation Time	**30 MIN.**
Cooking Time	**15 MIN.**
Method of cooking	**STOVETOP**
Microwave	**NO**
Freezing	**NO**
Keeping Time	**1 DAY**

SPECIAL NOTE

Bagna caôda is a typical recipe from Piedmont,
and comes from garlic-based recipes from popular
medieval cooking (such as Provençal *aïoli*,
Ligurian *agliata* and others).

RECOMMENDED WINES
Colline novaresi Bonarda (Piedmont): light red wine served at 61°F / 16°C
Barbera d'Alba superiore (Piedmont): light red wine served at 64°F / 18°C

1 Melt the butter in a fondue pot or chaffing dish over a heat source.
Add the thinly sliced garlic and let it sauté without browning. When
it begins to fall apart, add the anchovy fillets and pour in the oil a
little at a time. Mix with a wooden spoon slowly, always in the same
direction. The *bagna caôda* should simmer for about 10 minutes, and
the anchovies should dissolve completely (be careful not to allow to
sauce to boil). When everything is well-blended, serve with the
chaffing dish still over flame.

2 The way various types of vegetables offered to your guests are
presented on the platter is very important; they must be dipped into
the *bagna caôda*, which is placed in the middle of the table.

3 The cardoons should be trimmed of threads, and you should use
the most tender stalks. If they darken, place them in a bath of water
and lemon juice. The peppers should be cleaned well and chopped,
after you remove the stem, the seeds and the inner ribs.

4 The Jerusalem artichokes should be peeled and sliced thinly. The
celery should be cut into stalks, keeping the most tender ones, and
the fennel should be cut into wedges, with only the hearts showing
on the table.

PRACTICAL SUGGESTIONS
ʃ *you want the odor of garlic to be less intense, slice it thinly and then soak
it in milk for a couple of hours before using it. Drain it, dry and cook.*

Spinach Strudel

INGREDIENTS

serves 4

For the filling

2.2 lb. − I kg SPINACH
SALT to taste
1/2 lb. − 200 g ROMAN RICOTTA
I pinch NUTMEG
2 tablespoons GRATED PARMESAN

For the dough

2 cups − 200 g WHITE FLOUR
pinch of SALT, 2 EGGS

For the seasoning

1/8 cup − 30 g MELTED BUTTER
2 leaves SAGE, I clove GARLIC
3 tablespoons GRATED PARMESAN

EQUIPMENT

an oval pot with a cover, a mixing bowl
a rolling pin, a serving dish

Difficulty	ELABORATE
Preparation Time	I HOUR
Cooking Time	35 MIN.
Method of cooking	STOVETOP
Microwave	NO
Freezing	YES
Keeping Time	2 DAYS

SPECIAL NOTE

Nutmeg is indispensable in Middle Eastern
cooking. It can be toxic if consumed in large
doses. It has long been used as a soporific in
calming drinks.

RECOMMENDED WINES
Collio goriziano Merlot (Friuli–Venezia Giulia):
light red wine served at 64°F / 18°C
Oltrepò Pavese rosso (Lombardy): light red wine served at 64°F / 18°C

I Clean and wash the spinach, place in a pot with only the draining water, salt it and cook about 5 minutes. Run it immediately under cold water, squeeze, mince, place in a mixing bowl, add the ricotta, cheese and nutmeg, and mix with a wooden spoon to blend the ingredients.

2 Prepare the pastry. Mound the flour on a flat surface with a pinch of salt, add the eggs and knead until you have a smooth mixture. Roll it out thinly into an oval shape. Place the prepared filling on it and roll up the pastry into a roll. Seal the two ends.

3 Place the oval pot on the heat with salted water, bring to a boil, add the strudel, cover and cook over moderate heat about 20 minutes.

4 In the meantime, brown the butter in a small frying pan with the sage and, if you like, garlic. When the strudel is done, remove from the pot and let it sit for 3 minutes, then transfer to a heated serving dish, cut into slices, sprinkle with cheese and dot with butter, and serve immediately.

PRACTICAL SUGGESTIONS
To make this dish lighter, we suggest sprinkling with parmesan, but seasoning only with raw butter, which will melt on contact with the strudel (as for cheese and spinach ravioli).

Baked Zucchini

INGREDIENTS

serves 4

1 3/4 lb. – 700 g ZUCCHINI
1 sprig PARSLEY
1 sprig BASIL
2 cloves GARLIC
3/4 lb. – 250 g MOZZARELLA
EXTRA VIRGIN OLIVE OIL as necessary
SALT and PEPPER to taste
TOMATO SAUCE as necessary
4 tablespoons GRATED PARMESAN
1 oz. – 20 g BUTTER

EQUIPMENT

a pot
a baking dish

Difficulty	AVERAGE
Preparation Time	15 MIN.
Cooking Time	40 MIN.
Method of cooking	OVEN
Microwave	YES
Freezing	YES
Keeping Time	3 DAYS

SPECIAL NOTE

When zucchini still have their yellow flowers, it's a good sign that they are fresh and have no seeds inside.

RECOMMENDED WINES
Colli Tortonesi Cortese (Piedmont):
mellow, aromatic white wine served at 50°F / 10°C
Ischia rosso (Campania): light red wine served at 54°F / 12°C

1 Wash the zucchini, and without peeling, cut them lengthwise into slices about a quarter inch – half a centimeter in width. Add them to a pot of boiling water and cook 3 minutes, then drain well. Trim and wash the parsley and basil and mince them with the garlic. Chop the mozzarella into small pieces.

2 Place a layer of zucchini in a lightly oiled baking dish, sprinkle with the aromatic minced mixture, add a pinch of salt and pepper, place the pieces of mozzarella on top, drizzle everything with the tomato sauce and a tablespoon oil, then sprinkle with grated parmesan. Make a second layer of zucchini and continue in this way until the ingredients are finished. Dot the top with butter.

3 Place the baking dish in a preheated 350°F oven and bake about 40 minutes. When done, let it sit in the oven for about 3 more minutes, then remove and serve piping hot in the baking dish.

PRACTICAL SUGGESTIONS

When you buy zucchini, select small ones, because the larger ones are usually full of seeds that you'll have to remove. To prevent them from absorbing too much water when they're boiling, you can cut them into small pieces and steam cook.

Florentine Pie

INGREDIENTS
serves 4

1 1/3 lb. ZUCCHINI
WHITE FLOUR as necessary
SUNFLOWER SEED OIL for frying
SALT to taste
3 EGGS
4 tablespoons MILK
a pinch MARJORAM
a handful minced PARSLEY

EQUIPMENT
a frying pan
absorbent paper towels
a baking dish

Difficulty	AVERAGE
Preparation Time	15 MIN.
Cooking Time	40 MIN.
Method of cooking	STOVETOP AND OVEN
Microwave	YES
Freezing	YES
Keeping Time	2 DAYS

SPECIAL NOTE
Zucchini are the fruit of several varieties of squash that are harvested as soon as they begin to develop. The species cultivated for this purpose is *Cucurbita pepo.*

RECOMMENDED WINES
Vernaccia di San Gimignano (Tuscany):
mellow, aromatic white wine served at 50°F / 10°C
Capri bianco (Campania): dry white wine served at 57°F / 14°C

1 Trim, wash, dry and slice the zucchini lengthwise, lightly flour them and fry in a frying pan in a generous amount of hot, but not smoking oil, a few at a time. Drain when they have turned golden brown on both sides, and place them on absorbent paper towels to eliminate any excess oil.

2 Arrange them in layers in a baking dish, and add salt. Break the eggs in a mixing bowl, beat with the milk, marjoram, parsley and a pinch of salt, then pour the mixture on the zucchini.

3 Bake in a preheated 350°F oven for about twenty minutes. The pie should be soft in the center. Serve hot in the baking dish.

PRACTICAL SUGGESTIONS
You can make an excellent pie by steaming whole zucchini instead of frying them as indicated, then cutting them lengthwise when they're done. The pie will be better balanced nutritionally.

Cabbage and Potatoes

Colli Morenici Mantovani del Garda rosso (Lombardy):
light red wine served at 61°F / 16°C
San Colombano Rosso (Lombardy): light red wine served at 61°F / 16°C

1 Wash, trim and slice the cabbage into strips. Wash and peel the potatoes, but leave them whole. Place the vegetables in a pot and cover with cold salted water. Cook about 40 minutes, carefully drain the cabbage and mash the hot potatoes.

2 Place the cabbage and mashed potatoes in a large mixing bowl. Peel and crush a clove of garlic, and wash and dry the rosemary. Place everything in a frying pan with the olive oil, just barely heat, then add the contents of the mixing bowl. Season for several minutes and adjust the salt.

3 Cut the slices of bread in two and toast in the oven. Peel the remaining clove of garlic, cut in two and remove the green shoot in the center. Rub the cut side on the toasted bread. Place the bread on the serving dish and pour the vegetables over it. Serve piping hot.

INGREDIENTS

serves 4

2.2 lb. – 1 kg CABBAGE
4 POTATOES
SALT to taste
2 cloves GARLIC
2 sprigs ROSEMARY
4 tablespoon EXTRA VIRGIN OLIVE OIL
4 slices HOMEMADE BREAD

EQUIPMENT

a pot
a mixing bowl
a serving dish

Difficulty	AVERAGE
Preparation Time	25 MIN.
Cooking Time	45 MIN.
Method of cooking	STOVETOP AND OVEN
Microwave	NO
Freezing	NO
Keeping Time	1 DAY

PRACTICAL SUGGESTIONS
The best way to clean the cabbage leaves of earth and insects, is immerse them in water acidulated with lemon juice for about ten minutes. If you want to minimize the odor of the cabbage as it cooks, place a cloth moistened with strong vinegar on the pot cover.

SPECIAL NOTE
For bronchitis, boil a cabbage leaf without ribs in a cup of milk. Filter it, sweeten with honey, and drink a hot cup of it two or three times a day.

Chard Stalks Parmesan

INGREDIENTS

serves 4

1 lb. – 500 g CHARD STALKS
SALT to taste
WHITE FLOUR as necessary
SUNFLOWER SEED OIL for frying
a walnut–sized chunk of BUTTER
6 tablespoons GRATED PECORINO

For the sauce

1 lb. – 400 g SAUCE TOMATOES
1 ONION
4 tablespoons EXTRA VIRGIN OLIVE OIL
1/3 lb. – 150 g GROUND MEAT
SALT and PEPPER to taste

EQUIPMENT

absorbent paper towels
a pot, a frying pan
a small saucepan, a baking dish

Difficulty	AVERAGE
Preparation Time	20 MIN.
Cooking Time	1 HOUR 20 MIN.
Method of cooking	STOVETOP AND OVEN
Microwave	YES
Freezing	YES
Keeping Time	3 DAYS

SPECIAL NOTE

Chard originated in the Mediterranean basin. Once only the leaves were consumed, which the Romans enjoyed primarily in soups.

Recommended Wines
Torgiano rosso (Umbria): light red wine served at 57°F / 14°C
San Severo rosato (Puglia): rosé served at 54°F / 12°C

1 Wash the chard stalks, trim and remove the green portion and the threads. Then cut into pieces 2–2.5 inches – 5–6 centimeters long, and boil in a pot with a generous amount of salted water about 10 minutes, to very al dente. Drain, cool and flour. Place a generous amount of oil into a frying pan, and when it is very hot, add the floured stalks, browning them well on all sides. Drain, place on absorbent paper towels and set aside.

2 Prepare the sauce. Toss the tomatoes into boiling water, drain after a few minutes, peel, remove the seeds and vegetable water and chop. Peel the onion, mince it and sauté it well in a small saucepan with extra virgin olive oil and the ground meat, stirring occasionally with a wooden spoon, then add a pinch of salt and freshly ground pepper, add the tomatoes, and cook over low heat, covered, for 40–50 minutes, adding a bit of broth if necessary.

3 Butter a baking dish, place a layer of chard stalks on it, then one of sauce and a sprinkling of pecorino, then continue layering until the ingredients are finished. The last layer should be sauce and pecorino. Bake at 340°F for about 15 minutes. Serve hot.

Practical Suggestions
The chard leaves that are not used in this dish can be used to make a delicate rice soup, or you can steam them and sauté them in a small amount of butter.

102

Au Gratin Tomatoes

INGREDIENTS

serves 4

8 firm ripe TOMATOES
1 sprig PARSLEY
a few BASIL leaves
1 ONION
1 tablespoon SALTED CAPERS
1 pinch OREGANO
4 tablespoons BREAD CRUMBS
SALT and PEPPER to taste
4 tablespoons EXTRA VIRGIN OLIVE OIL

EQUIPMENT

a mixing bowl
a baking dish
a serving dish

Difficulty	AVERAGE
Preparation Time	45 MIN.
Cooking Time	45 MIN.
Method of cooking	OVEN
Microwave	YES
Freezing	NO
Keeping Time	1 DAY

SPECIAL NOTE

Tomatoes are native to South America, probably Peru, where they have been cultivated since ancient times. They were imported to Europe in the 16th century, but only became common in the 19th century.

RECOMMENDED WINES
Val d'Arbia (Tuscany): dry white wine served at 50°F / 10°C
Laverano bianco (Puglia): dry white wine served at 50°F / 10°C

1 Wash and dry the tomatoes, slice off the top and remove the seeds, place upside down over a sieve and let them drain for about a half hour, until they lose their vegetable liquid. Trim and wash the sprig of parsley. Wash the basil leaves and dry them with a dishcloth. Peel the onion and, using a chopping knife, mince them with the parsley and basil.

2 Place the minced mixture in a mixing bowl, add the washed and dried capers, the oregano, 3 tablespoons bread crumbs, a pinch of salt, a grind of pepper and a tablespoon extra virgin olive oil. Mix everything well with a wooden spoon until the ingredients are well blended.

3 Finally, transfer the tomatoes to a flat surface, with the cut portion upward. Fill with the prepared mixture and sprinkle with the remaining bread crumbs.

4 Lightly oil a baking dish and add the tomatoes. Drizzle with the remaining oil and bake about 45 minutes in an oven preheated to 320°F, or until the surface has lightly browned. When done, remove from the oven, transfer to a serving dish and serve hot or cold.

PRACTICAL SUGGESTIONS
Basil, oregano, capers: sometimes all you need are a few ingredients with an intense flavor and few or no calories to make a simple dish a delicacy. This is the secret of Mediterranean cooking.

Mushroom Croquettes

INGREDIENTS

serves 4

1 large handful – 40 g STALE SOFT BREAD CRUMBS

2 cloves GARLIC

1 sprig PARSLEY

3/4 lb. – 300 g GROUND BEEF

3 tablespoons EXTRA VIRGIN OLIVE OIL

1 lb. – 500 g PORCINI MUSHROOMS

4 tablespoons GRATED PECORINO

SALT and PEPPER to taste

3 EGGS

CORN OIL for frying

EQUIPMENT

a bowl, a small saucepan

a saucepan, a mixing bowl

a frying pan

absorbent paper towels

a serving dish

Difficulty	**AVERAGE**
Preparation Time	**20 MIN.**
Cooking Time	**30 MIN.**
Method of cooking	**STOVETOP**
Microwave	**NO**
Freezing	**NO**
Keeping Time	**2 DAYS**

SPECIAL NOTE

Because certain mushrooms contain hallucinogenic substances, magical powers have been attributed to them, and even today some populations use them during special ceremonies.

RECOMMENDED WINES

Colli Altotiberini rosso (Umbria): ligh ted wine served at 57°F / 14°C

Oltrepò Pavese rosso (Lombardy): light red wine served at 61°F / 16°C

1 Soak the stale bread crumbs for about ten minutes in a bowl of lukewarm water or vegetable broth, squeeze well and mince. Peel the garlic, wash and trim the parsley and mince it. Place the ground beef in a small saucepan with the olive oil and sauté about 10 minutes.

2 Clean the mushrooms with a damp cloth, chop, place in a saucepan (nonstick is best) without adding any seasoning, and dry out the vegetable water over low heat. Transfer to a mixing bowl and let them cool. Add the ground beef, the bread crumbs, the aromatic minced mixture and the pecorino. Add a pinch of salt and freshly ground pepper and break the eggs over it. Thoroughly blend everything with a wooden spoon, and form numerous small croquettes from the mixture.

3 Place corn oil in a frying pan, and when it is very hot, add the croquettes. Let them brown well on all sides, them remove them, place them on absorbent paper towels to eliminate any excess oil, transfer to a serving dish, surround with a few leaves of curly lettuce, and serve warm.

PRACTICAL SUGGESTIONS

If you can't find fresh mushrooms, use frozen or dried ones instead. Remember that to obtain the same degree of flavor, 1/2 ounce – 15 grams dry mushrooms are the same as about 12 ounces – 300 grams fresh mushrooms.

Eggplant Parmesan

INGREDIENTS

serves 4

1 1/3 lb. – 600 g EGGPLANTS
SALT to taste
2 tablespoons WHITE FLOUR
SUNFLOWER SEED OIL for frying
half an ONION
6 tablespoons EXTRA VIRGIN OLIVE OIL
6 small BASIL leaves
1/2 lb. – 200 g MOZZARELLA, sliced thinly
3/4 lb. – 300 g TOMATOES, peeled and seeded
4 tablespoons – 70 g GRATED PARMESAN

EQUIPMENT

a frying pan
a saucepan
absorbent paper towels
a baking dish

Difficulty	AVERAGE
Preparation Time	30 MIN.
Cooking Time	50 MIN.
Method of cooking	STOVETOP AND OVEN
Microwave	YES
Freezing	YES
Keeping Time	3 DAYS

SPECIAL NOTE

Eggplant is a member of the Solanaceae family. It
is probably a native of India, and is now
cultivated in many Mediterranean countries.

RECOMMENDED WINES
Rosato del Salento (Campania): rosé served at 57°F / 14°C
Alcamo bianco (Sicily): dry white wine served at 50°F / 10°C

1 Wash the eggplants, dry them and slice lengthwise. Place on a slanted board, sprinkle with salt and let them sit about an hour. Then run them under cold water, dry them and flour. Heat a generous amount of oil in the frying pan, and when it begins to smoke, brown the eggplant slices on both sides. Drain, place on absorbent paper towels to absorb any excess oil and set aside, keeping them warm. Finely mince the onion and sauté it in a saucepan with 3 tablespoons olive oil. Sieve the tomatoes, add to the onion, add a pinch of salt and freshly ground pepper and cook the sauce over low heat for 10 minutes. Then add the basil and cook another 5 minutes.

2 Oil a baking dish and make a layer of eggplant. Arrange the mozzarella slices on top to cover completely, pour a layer of tomato sauce over it and sprinkle with grated parmesan and a pinch of salt. Continue this way until the ingredients are finished, ending with mozzarella, tomato and cheese and sprinkling the surface with a bit of olive oil. Preheat the oven to 350°F and bake for 15 minutes, until the top becomes golden brown, then remove and serve immediately, piping hot, in the serving dish.

PRACTICAL SUGGESTIONS
You can vary this recipe by adding sliced hardboiled eggs or small fried meatballs. If you like a crunchier crust, sprinkle the surface with grated bread crumbs and dot with butter.

Stuffed Bell Peppers

INGREDIENTS
serves 4

4 large, fleshy BELL PEPPERS
2 salted ANCHOVIES
I sprig PARSLEY
I tablespoon CAPERS IN SALT
2 1/2 oz. – 60 g PITTED GREEN OLIVES
3/4 lb. – 300 g SOFT BREAD CRUMBS
4 heaping tablespoons – 80 g GRATED
PECORINO
4 tablespoons EXTRA VIRGIN OLIVE OIL
I lb. – 500 g TOMATO SAUCE
SALT and PEPPER to taste

EQUIPMENT
a mixing bowl
a baking pan
a serving dish

Difficulty	AVERAGE
Preparation Time	20 MIN.
Cooking Time	40 MIN.
Method of cooking	OVEN
Microwave	YES
Freezing	YES
Keeping Time	I MONTH

SPECIAL NOTE
In Italian, "to be like parsley" means to turn up everywhere. In fact, parsley is the most commonly used aromatic herb in the world, both fresh and dried.

RECOMMENDED WINES
San Severo bianco (Puglia): dry white wine served at 50°F / 10°C
Etna bianco (Sicily): dry white wine served at 50°F / 10°C

1 Wash the peppers and dry with a kitchen cloth, then cut in half lengthwise and remove the seeds and white parts, being careful not to break the peppers. Remove the salt from the anchovies, bone and mince them. Trim the parsley, wash it and mince it. Remove the salt from the capers, and chop the olives in half.

2 Soak the bread crumbs, squeeze them well and place in a mixing bowl. Add the pieces of anchovy, the pecorino, the olives, the capers, the parsley, 2 tablespoons oil, a few tablespoons tomato sauce, a pinch of salt and a bit of freshly ground pepper, and mix well with a wooden spoon until the ingredients are well blended.

3 Place the oil and remaining tomato sauce in a baking pan, add the peppers, which you have stuffed with the filling, and bake in an oven preheated to 350°F for about 40 minutes. When done, remove and transfer the peppers to a serving dish. Serve hot with the cooking sauce in its own gravy boat.

PRACTICAL SUGGESTIONS
Select different colored bell peppers for a lively presentation. Before you stuff them, you can blacken them over a flame and skin them, or else leave them as they are, and your guests can remove the skin.

Stuffed Cabbage

INGREDIENTS

serves 4

1 HEAD SAVOY CABBAGE, SALT to taste
1/4 lb. – 200 g GROUND PORK
1/4 lb. – 200 g GROUND VEAL
1/4 cup – 40 g BUTTER
1 sprig each THYME, MARJORAM and ROSEMARY
pinch OF NUTMEG
5 tablespoons DRY WHITE WINE
For the béchamel
1 oz. – 20 g BUTTER, 1 oz. – 20 g WHITE
FLOUR, 3 tablespoons – 1 dl MILK
SALT and PEPPER to taste
For the sauce
2 EGG YOLKS, 1/2 cup CREAM
3 tablespoons FLOUR, SALT to taste

EQUIPMENT

a skillet, a frying pan
2 small saucepans, a baking dish
a double boiler

Difficulty	**AVERAGE**
Preparation Time	**30 MIN.**
Cooking Time	**2 HOURS**
Method of cooking	**STOVETOP AND OVEN**
Microwave	**YES**
Freezing	**NO**
Keeping Time	**1 DAY**

SPECIAL NOTE

Savoy cabbage *(Brassica oleracea* var. *sabauda)* is
a late fall–winter vegetable. Like cauliflower,
tradition has it that it is tastier when
exposed to frost.

RECOMMENDED WINES

Torgiano rosso (Umbria): light red wine served at 64°F / 18°C
Ghemme (Piedmont): medium–bodied red wine served at 64°F / 18°C

1 Wash the cabbage and eliminate the hard outer leaves. Bring salted water to boil in a skillet and cook the cabbage whole for 10 minutes. Place the meats in a frying pan with two tablespoons butter, the herbs and seasonings, salt and cook for 20 minutes, moistening with white wine. Prepare the béchamel. Melt the butter in a small saucepan, add the flour and stir until you have a smooth sauce. Mix a third of the milk and 3 tablespoons water, and stirring constantly, add to the mixture. When the mixture begins to thicken, little by little add the remaining milk and 2 tablespoons water. Add salt and pepper and cook for 15 minutes, stirring constantly.

2 Drain the cabbage, spread the leaves and stuff it with spoonfuls of meat (after removing the herbs) and béchamel, close but not mixed together. Tie it with twine, place in a baking pan with the remaining butter and bake in a preheated 350°F oven for an hour. Moisten with a bit of broth if necessary. When done, remove the cabbage and let it cool to lukewarm. In the meantime, prepare the sauce. Place the egg yolks in a small saucepan with the cream, cook over a double boiler, mixing and being careful not to let it grow lumpy. Slowly add the flour and salt. Untie the cabbage and cut it into thick slices, place them on individual plates, add the sauce and serve.

PRACTICAL SUGGESTIONS

The hard ribs of cabbage leaves should be eliminated before cooking. The smaller ribs, left whole and boiled with the other ingredients and then discarded, will make soups more flavorful.

Stuffed Endive Bundles

1 Trim the endive well, remove any damaged leaves, wash and drain well. Place the pitted black olives in a mixing bowl, add the plum tomatoes, sliced thinly, the mozzarella cut into small cubes, the minced anchovy fillets, the minced parsley and the oregano.

2 Season everything with a pinch of salt and a bit of freshly ground pepper, drizzle with the oil and mix the ingredients well. Open each head of endive very gently, then stuff them with a bit of the prepared mixture. Shape them again and tie each head with the kitchen thread.

3 Melt the butter in a frying pan, add the minced onion, let it brown gently, then place the stuffed endive heads in the sauce. Sauté them uniformly, then slowly moisten them with a bit of hot broth and continue cooking for about 20–25 minutes.

4 Sprinkle the surface with the grated gruyere, turn off the heat, cover the pan and let it sit for a few minutes. Transfer the bundles to the serving dish and serve.

PRACTICAL SUGGESTIONS
To make the filling for this dish more substantial, you can add 6 oz. – 150 grams tuna in oil, or the same amount of finely minced lean ham.

INGREDIENTS

serves 4

4 ENDIVE HEADS
3 oz. – 80 g PITTED BLACK OLIVES, slivered
4 PLUM TOMATOES, peeled and seeded
1 FRESH MOZZARELLA
8 ANCHOVY FILLETS WITH THE SALT REMOVED
1 sprig PARSLEY, minced
1 pinch OREGANO
SALT and PEPPER to taste
2 tablespoons EXTRA VIRGIN OLIVE OIL
1/4 cup – 50 g BUTTER
1 ONION
1 cup VEGETABLE BROTH
3 tablespoons GRATED GRUYÈRE

EQUIPMENT

a mixing bowl, a frying pan
kitchen thread, a serving dish

Difficulty	AVERAGE
Preparation Time	20 MIN.
Cooking Time	30 MIN.
Method of cooking	STOVETOP
Microwave	YES
Freezing	NO
Keeping Time	2 DAYS

SPECIAL NOTE

Gruyère is a typical denomination cheese that is a specialty of the Swiss cheese industry. It takes its name from its town of origin, Gruyères, which is located in the rocky spurs of the foothills of the Alps near Fribourg.

Leeks with Cheese

INGREDIENTS

serves 4

2.2 lb. – I kg LEEKS
EXTRA VIRGIN OLIVE OIL as necessary
2 heaping tablespoons – 50 g GRATED PARMESAN
I tablespoon – 15 g BUTTER
SALT as necessary

For the sauce

4 tablespoons – 30 g BUTTER
1/2 cup – 60 g WHITE FLOUR
I 1/2 cups VEGETABLE BROTH
SALT to taste
3 tablespoons – 60 g GRATED PARMESAN

EQUIPMENT

a skillet
a baking dish

Difficulty	AVERAGE
Preparation Time	30 MIN.
Cooking Time	45 MIN.
Method of cooking	STOVETOP AND OVEN
Microwave	YES
Freezing	YES
Keeping Time	2 DAYS

SPECIAL NOTE

The leek is a member of the Liliaceae family. It is a native of Mediterranean countries and is cultivated for its fleshy, elongated bulb, which is eaten as a vegetable.

RECOMMENDED WINES
*Genazzano bianco (Lazio): dry white wine served at 50°F / 10°C
Albana di Romagna secco (Emilia Romagna):
mellow, aromatic white wine served at 50°F / 10°C*

I Remove the green portion and the roots of the leeks, and discard the hard outer leaves as well. Cut the leeks in half lengthwise and carefully wash under running water. Then cut into pieces about an inch – 2 centimeters long and arrange in an oiled baking dish.

2 Prepare the cheese sauce. Melt the butter in a skillet, add the flour, and stirring constantly with a wooden spoon, cook for a few minutes, being careful not to allow the flour to brown.

3 Then add the boiling vegetable broth, continue stirring with a wooden spoon and cook about 10 minutes. Season with a pinch of salt and grated parmesan.

4 Pour the sauce uniformly over the leeks, sprinkle with grated parmesan and dot with a bit of butter. Bake in a preheated 350°F oven about 30 minutes. Serve piping hot in the baking dish.

PRACTICAL SUGGESTIONS
For this dish to be successful, the leeks must be at least 10–12 inches – 25–30 centimeters long, with the white part extended by 1/3 or half of the sheathed portion, and a diameter of 1–1 ½ inches – 2–3 centimeters. Yellowed or wilted tips are an indication of poor quality.

Potato Pie

INGREDIENTS

serves 4

2 lb. – 800 g POTATOES
2/3 lb. – 250 g MUSHROOMS
2 tablespoons EXTRA VIRGIN OLIVE OIL
1 clove GARLIC
1 teaspoon minced PARSLEY
SALT and PEPPER to taste
1/4 cup – 60 g BUTTER
1 cup MILK
1 EGG
1/4 lb. – 100 g GRATED CHEESE
2 tablespoons – 50 g WHITE FLOUR

EQUIPMENT

a pot, a potato ricer
a mixing bowl, a saucepan
a blender or chopping knife
a baking dish

Difficulty	AVERAGE
Preparation Time	20 MIN.
Cooking Time	1 HOUR 30 MIN.
Method of cooking	STOVETOP AND OVEN
Microwave	YES
Freezing	NO
Keeping Time	1 DAY

SPECIAL NOTE

Potatoes are traditionally indispensable to the diets of northern Europe, especially in German cooking.

RECOMMENDED WINES
Colli Albani (Lazio): dry white wine served at 50°F / 10°C
Breganze bianco (Veneto): dry white wine served at 50°F / 10°C

❖

1 Boil the potatoes in their skins in the pot, and when done, peel and rice. Place the mashed potatoes in a mixing bowl.

2 Carefully clean the mushrooms, wash them, chop into thin slices and cook 20 minutes in a saucepan with the oil, garlic, minced parsley, a pinch of salt and freshly ground pepper. When done, put through the blender or mince with the chopping knife.

3 Add the softened butter, the lukewarm milk, and a pinch of salt to the potatoes. Mix everything to obtain a thick, uniform puree. Add the mushrooms, the egg, the cheese and the flour. Mix all ingredients well with a wooden spoon to blend thoroughly.

4 Butter and flour the baking dish, add the prepared mixture and smooth the surface well. Bake 25–30 minutes in a preheated 350°F oven, or until the surface is golden brown. Serve piping hot in the baking dish.

PRACTICAL SUGGESTIONS
You can also use dried porcini mushrooms for this recipe. If you do, use about 1.5 oz. – 30 grams, and remember to soak them about 20 minutes in lukewarm water before cooking.

116

Cavolata

INGREDIENTS

serves 4

2.2 lb. – 1 kg CAULIFLOWER
2 oz. – 40 g SLAB BACON
1 ONION
4 tablespoons EXTRA VIRGIN OLIVE OIL
1 lb. – 400 g TOMATO SAUCE
SALT to taste

EQUIPMENT

a skillet
a serving dish

Difficulty	AVERAGE
Preparation Time	20 MIN.
Cooking Time	30 MIN.
Method of cooking	STOVETOP
Microwave	YES
Freezing	NO
Keeping Time	2 DAYS

SPECIAL NOTE

Cauliflower is a cold weather vegetable and is not damaged by frost. You can find it all year round, but its best season is between November and February, because frost makes it more firm and solid.

RECOMMENDED WINES

Cannonau di Sardegna rosato (Sardegna): rosé served at 57°F / 12°C
Dolcetto di Dogliani (Piedmont): light red wine served at 61°F / 16°C

1 Trim the cauliflower and break into florets, then carefully wash under running water and drain well. Cut the slab of bacon into cubes. Peel the onion, wash it, mince it and fry it over moderate heat in a skillet, being careful not to brown it too much.

2 As soon as the onion is golden brown, add the cauliflower florets and the diced bacon, mixing often with a wooden spoon.

3 Then add the tomato sauce, barely cover with water, season with salt and cook covered over very low heat for about 20 minutes.

4 When done, if the water is not completely absorbed, allow it to evaporate completely by raising the heat, then transfer to a serving dish and serve piping hot.

PRACTICAL SUGGESTIONS

To be sure a cauliflower is fresh when you buy it, check to see that it is perfectly white on the surface and is compact and solid. Any little leaves at the base of the flower should be hard and deep green in color. If they are yellowed or wilted, the cauliflower is old.

Squash with Beans

INGREDIENTS

serves 4

1 lb. – 400 g KIDNEY BEANS
SALT to taste
1 lb. – 400 g POTATOES
1 lb. – 400 g SQUASH, CLEANED
1 ONION
3 tablespoons EXTRA VIRGIN OLIVE OIL

EQUIPMENT

3 pots
a skillet
a serving dish

Difficulty	AVERAGE
Preparation Time	20 MIN.
Cooking Time	2 HOURS 50 MIN.
Method of cooking	STOVETOP
Microwave	NO
Freezing	NO
Keeping Time	1 DAY

SPECIAL NOTE

In northern Italy, squash is often combined with beans, spinach and potatoes. This recipe is especially typical of Friuli—Venezia Giulia.

RECOMMENDED WINES
Friuli Grave rosato (Friuli Venezia Giulia): rosé served at 54°F / 12°C
Santa Margherita di Belice bianco (Sicily) served at 50°F / 10°C

1 Wash the beans and cook in a large pot to which you have added cold salted water, for about an hour and a half. Wash the potatoes and boil in another pot to which you have added cold salted water, for about 40 minutes. Calculate your time from when the water begins to boil. Cook the squash in another pot of salted boiling water, for about 20 minutes.

2 When the vegetables are cooked, drain them, then peel the potatoes and slice them not too thinly, and cut the squash into cubes or slices. Peel the onion, mince it and fry over medium heat in a casserole with the oil.

3 Add all the boiled vegetables to the fried onion, adjust the salt if necessary, and season about 20 minutes, gently mixing with a wooden spoon. When done, transfer the mixture to a serving dish and serve piping hot.

PRACTICAL SUGGESTIONS
To prevent the squash from absorbing too much water while cooking, it's better to steam it for 15 minutes, or, after slicing into pieces about 1 1/4 inches — 3 centimeters thick, you can bake it in a preheated 400°F oven for 20–30 minutes. When it's done, you can cut it into cubes and proceed as indicated in the recipe.

Mushroom Caps on Grape Leaves

INGREDIENTS

serves 4

12 FIELD MUSHROOM CAPS
2 oz. – 1 bunch PARSLEY
3 cloves GARLIC
SALT to taste
EXTRA VIRGIN OLIVE OIL as necessary
12 GRAPE LEAVES

EQUIPMENT

a chopping knife
a baking dish
a serving dish

Difficulty	**EASY**
Preparation Time	**15 MIN.**
Cooking Time	**15 MIN.–20 MIN.**
Method of cooking	**OVEN**
Microwave	**NO**
Freezing	**NO**
Keeping Time	**1 DAY**

SPECIAL NOTE

Grapevines are the most ancient climbing plant found in gardens. *Vitis vinifera* "Aplifolia" has incised leaves. *Vitis vinifera* "Purpurea" has red leaves that with time become the color of wine.

RECOMMENDED WINES
Dolcetto di Ovada (Piedmont): light red wine served at 61°F / 16°C
Colli Amerini novello (Umbria): rosé served at 57°F / 14°C

1 Clean the mushroom caps well with a damp dishtowel and dry on a dry cloth. Wash and dry the parsley, peel the garlic, and using a chopping knife, finely mince them together.

2 Lightly oil a baking dish and place the mushrooms in it. Sprinkle each cap with the minced parsley and garlic and a pinch of salt, and drizzle the mushrooms with oil.

3 Cook in a preheated 350°F oven about 15–20 minutes. Arrange the mushrooms on a serving dish and place a thoroughly washed and dried grape leaf on each one. Serve.

PRACTICAL SUGGESTIONS
Rich and tasty, this is a true treat, especially when served with stuffed zucchini and tomatoes. You can also prepare it with very firm porcini mushroom caps, but remember that the recipe will cost you a lot more to make!